The Friendship of
Roland Barthes

The Friendship of Roland Barthes

Philippe Sollers
Translated by Andrew Brown

polity

First published in French as *L'amitié de Roland Barthes*, © Éditions du Seuil, 2015
This English edition © Polity Press, 2017

Polity Press
65 Bridge Street
Cambridge CB2 1UR, UK

Polity Press
350 Main Street
Malden, MA 02148, USA

ISBN-13: 978-1-5095-1331-4
ISBN-13: 978-1-5095-1332-1 (pb)

A catalogue record for this book is available from the British Library.

Library of Congress Cataloging-in-Publication Data

Names: Sollers, Philippe, 1936- author.
Title: The friendship of Roland Barthes / Philippe Sollers.
Other titles: Amiti?e de Roland Barthes. English
Description: Malden, MA : Polity Press, 2017. | Includes bibliographical
   references and index.
Identifiers: LCCN 2016029143| ISBN 9781509513314 (hardback) | ISBN
   9781509513321 (pbk.) | ISBN 9781509513352 (epub)
Subjects: LCSH: Barthes, Roland--Friends and associates. | Sollers, Philippe,
   1936---Friends and associates. | Barthes, Roland--Correspondence. |
   Sollers, Philippe, 1936---Correspondence. |
   Linguists--France--Correspondence. | Critics--France--Correspondence. |
   Authors, French--20th century--Correspondence.
Classification: LCC P85.B33 S6513 2017 | DDC 410.92 [B] --dc23 LC record available at
   https://lccn.loc.gov/2016029143

Typeset in 11pt on 14pt Sabon by
Servis Filmsetting Ltd, Stockport, Cheshire
Printed in Great Britain by CPI Group (UK) Ltd, Croydon

For further information on Polity, visit our website:
politybooks.com

Contents

Translator's Note

Sollers often refers to Barthes's texts without giving publication details or page numbers; I have translated all the quotations from Barthes afresh, with due thanks to the excellent translators who have served Barthes so well.

The pieces gathered in this small volume vary in style. 'Friendship' is a memoir in the form of an improvised monologue; 'R.B.' deploys the language of 1970s French intellectual polemic at its prickliest and most elliptically formulaic; the 'Appendices' look back, at times wryly, on the trip to China that Barthes and Sollers undertook, and also re-state Sollers's claim that Barthes's political analyses have lost none of their trenchancy in an age when a new mutation of Poujadism (paranoid, protectionist and xeno-phobic) is on the rise – and not just in France. Barthes's letters show a more intimate and unguarded side of him than we usually see: he was clearly an affectionate, loyal and caring friend. I have tried to stick fairly closely to the different tones in these pieces, with their sudden tangential breaks and occasional obscurities. I have kept annotation to a minimum: to explain what Sollers meant, in 1971, by 'dogmatico-revisionism', or to detail all the writers, publishers, academics and review editors mentioned by Sollers and Barthes, would involve a mini-history of French intellectual life since the 1960s. It seems less important to dwell on the doctrinal – or purely personal – polemics of forty years ago than to get a sense of why Sollers thinks that now, more than ever, might be a good time for us to be reminded of Barthes's lifelong and lucid awareness of the ever-present menace of terrorism.

FRIENDSHIP

The death of Roland Barthes, on 26 March 1980, came as a terrible shock to me, and it's still with me, it just won't go away. A word he loathed, referring to an event that he found heartrending – the death of his mother – was 'mourning'. *Mourning Diary* is a good title, but it's not about mourning. It's about what he called, using a word to which he restored its full force, 'sorrow'. Sorrow is completely different from mourning – which, the psychoanalytical accounts tell us, lasts two years, etc. I still experience this sorrow even today. Just as intensely as then. Sorrow, first of all, that this incident was obscured, in the news I initially received, by a great deal of uncertainty. It was practically as if it *must not* appear to be a fatal accident. I can still see and hear François Wahl saying: 'No, it's just a minor accident, he'll recover, he's absolutely fine.' Was it the lunch with François Mitterrand, who was elected French President the following year, that led to this cover-up? 'It's not serious!' As if Mitterrand had cast the evil eye on Barthes. I was finally informed that he was in a bad state, really bad – dying – and I just had time to go with Julia Kristeva and hold his hands. He recognized us, he said 'thank you'. We told him we loved him. But it was the end. I always found this odd because what we lack is a discourse by Barthes on Mitterrand, a 'mythology' of that future left-wing president. So presidents of France come and go but we don't have Barthes's account of this lunch – *his* account.

And while I'm on the topic of French presidents, I'll mention, if I may, the fact that when Julia Kristeva was decorated by Nicolas Sarkozy, he told her all of a sudden that she had been friends with Roland *Barthez* (*sic*). There was laughter in the audience, immediately stifled. All the same, this slip of the tongue depicts, in my view, the state of continual degradation in French political life and my feeling that we need to start again from scratch.

So we miss Barthes simply for his way of being, his body. He could play the piano; drawing came to his hands in a completely spontaneous way; his handwriting – it was a pleasure to see his writing in blue ink, his whole way of writing; then there was his voice, the timbre of his voice, his diction. . . Where are we now when it comes to voices? Who still has a voice? There are two, for me, obvious voices: first, Lacan when he started improvising (since he thought aloud, the fact of speaking gave him things to think about), and then Barthes: he starts writing but ultimately he finds things to write about because he's starting to write. It's all a matter of voices, in other words something inspired that transpires in a certain breathiness, a certain difficulty, in Barthes's case, due to the illness he had overcome, after a struggle. What we hear, stemming from all of this, is a very odd detachment.

The first text Barthes wrote on me dates back to 1965, in the review *Critique*, and it was about my book *Drame*. So that was fifty years ago. Has today's literary situation emerged from the desert of that period? Barthes is more contemporary and precise than ever and I am going to deliver a *political* encomium on him, since that's how he always perceived the bedrock of his life, namely the fact that literature grants us a quite particular way of looking at politics. As evidence, we can point to the very fine text he wrote as a young man on Plato's *Crito*, in which he imagines a Socrates who does not commit suicide – after all, things might have turned out differently, no one is obliged to commit suicide, to obey the laws of the city, to sacrifice him- or herself. In 1934, Barthes was nineteen, he was at the Lycée Louis-le-Grand and this was when, he says, he started a little literary review – it wasn't a literary review but an 'antifascist republican defence group called DRAF, which we set up to defend ourselves against the arrogance of the "patriotic" youth groups that were in the majority in the final year at school'. What are things like now?

Barthes: political through literature. Literature enables us to say things that are quite accurate and true about politics. Why? Well, this is Barthes's immediate work in a nutshell: how can we avoid the stereotype, the cliché? The world tells lies, commodities are a lie. See Barthes's early work *Mythologies* (which, by the way, ought to be redone, since Barthes's intention is ageless; we ought to write a *Mythologies* for today*). And so, in 1957, as a

---

* There have in fact been several analyses of contemporary culture in the style or spirit of Barthes, both in France and elsewhere, including Peter Conrad's series of 'Twenty-First Century Mythologies' on BBC Radio 4, broadcast in the

barely known writer, Barthes published a droll little book, cold, quirky, insolent, corrosive, *Mythologies*. His aim was to describe, at a distance, the social comedy, so as better to neutralize it. The method isn't all that different from one of Gulliver's travels, except that the Lilliputians, here, are the prisoners of spontaneous beliefs and superstitions that are, perhaps, still ours. You might think that all this is very distant, as we have lived through so many transformations and changes. Far from it. Let's take one concrete example: Poujadism.* A permanent, specifically French grimace, still at work, now and always. And as far as the rest goes, literary criticism, magazines and weeklies (*Elle, Paris Match*, etc.), legends and icons, theatrical spectacles of every kind: it all hangs together, and we're discovering that we live in an order that claims to be natural but is, in every way, intensely deliberate. But there are no big words in Barthes; there's no anathema, no preaching, no denunciation: all the force of the demonstration lies in the apparently neutral description. It's humiliating for a society to be exposed to itself like this, and the greatest insult we can inflict on society is to tell it that we don't believe it. So Barthes has, right from the start, a bad reputation. There's the lie of illusion, there are lies everywhere, and Barthes is the first to sense that the age of the Spectacle is dawning. And we need to become aware of this. These texts are absolutely essential: society is a spectacle and so is politics, where everyone lies more often than not, with endlessly repeated words, i.e. an ideology which imbues everything – and we need to turn this ideology on its back and describe it – and what Barthes calls the 'sticky' (what a lovely word!), namely everything that weighs, bogs, slows you down, makes things too noisy. And above all there's 'babble' – a magnificent invention, the Tower of Babel, the Tower of Babble. There's already the chatter of Barthes's own time, so what are we to say about nowadays? It's been multiplied ten thousand fold!

All that sticky, nihilistic stuff is, quite simply, a way of evading reality. It's a huge drug. I'm very pleased that in one letter he bestows on me the title of 'great stimulating Drug'.* It's true that our lives were completely different. What he spotted in me right from the start was the fact that, from a very early age, I'd begun to lead a very free and restless life, while in his case this was something that caught up with him at the end, in a rather terrible way, it has to be said.

A little politics straight away, since I believe that it's necessary today: an interview for a magazine. We're in 1978 and it's especially interesting as it's an interview for *Elle*, which had been given a very sarcastic mention in *Mythologies* and, like all magazines in fact, ought to be discussed again, with even darker sarcasm, in a new series of mythologies. While we're on the subject, before reading the passage relating to the situation in 1978 – as you'll see, it's just like today – let's talk about *Le Monde* which, as you know, waged an absolutely frenzied campaign against Barthes's *On Racine*, and defended its own

---

* Letter of 25 August 1973 (see p. 103 below). (Translator's note.)

anti-Barthes champion: step forward, Raymond Picard! This was the 'Picard affair', the '*On Racine* affair'. If we re-read what people wrote at the time, it's staggering! It's neither more nor less than demanding someone's death: he should have his head chopped off, quick as you can, and how dare he come along and disturb our little habits . . . ! It's nothing like 1968 when there was turmoil in the university system; it was like a pressure cooker already on the point of exploding, as the Racine affair proved. It was extraordinary in its violence. There followed a lengthy press campaign, and it was amazingly relentless. It was open warfare, right from the start. In any case, literature *is* war. What else could it be? You tell me! Barthes was fully aware of the fact. Literature is war.

In 1978, here's what Roland Barthes says:

> The future can never be fully predicted. But any reading of the present does allow us to reckon upon all the fears and threats of the days to come. Latent anti-Semitism, like all forms of racism in every country, every civilization, every mentality, is still thriving in petit-bourgeois ideology. In France, fortunately, it is not supported by any significant political decisions. But the temptation of anti-Semitism and racism is evident in the press and in conversations. The fact that it's a reality on the ideological level means that intellectuals need to be very vigilant. This is where they have a positive role to play. [. . .] I think that, in the face of all these dangers, the right thing – i.e., hope – is always on the side of the marginal.

We may note in passing that hope as a definition of the right thing is surprising and interesting.

But what is emblematic is the idea of a combat on an individual scale. There's no one less gregarious, less communitarian than Barthes. There are his friends, there's a circle of friends, and sometimes there's a bosom friend who has the right to a personal meeting, while not sharing the same lifestyle or having the same tendencies when it comes to bodily enjoyment. Basically I'm the only heterosexual man to have had the benefit of representing something for Barthes to such a degree. I'm not saying that he didn't have other heterosexual friends, of course, but at this point, where we're in a situation of mass communitarianism, I'd like to underline all the same the beginning of *Sollers Writer* – it's important for today, given the fact that it was written in 1979, on 6 January:

> The writer is alone, abandoned by the old classes and the new. His fall is all the more grave in that he now lives in a society where solitude itself is essentially considered to be a failing. We accept (and this is our magisterial ploy) particularisms, but not singularities; types, but not individuals. We create (in a brilliant and cunning manoeuvre) choruses of particulars, all with their protesting, shrill, inoffensive voices. But what about the absolutely isolated person – who is neither Breton, nor Corsican, nor a woman, nor a homosexual, nor mad, nor an Arab, etc? Who does not *even* belong to a minority? Literature is this person's voice [. . .].

Well, that's pretty clear, isn't it? Very well written, to begin with, like everything he wrote. Singularity, that's what he's after.

I can still see us, Julia Kristeva and me, in the courtyard of the hospital of La Pitié-Salpêtrière. We had just bidden him farewell and we were really crushed under our *sorrow*. Roland liked Julia very much, as is shown by a magnificent text that he wrote about her at a time when she was absolutely blacklisted; it's called 'The Foreigner'. And she told me – she has since become a very good psychoanalyst: 'Basically, he has gone to join his mother.' The *sorrow* of Barthes's final days, when nobody could understand his sorrow! Here, he realizes that human beings are brutal, that they lack imagination. 'So yeah, okay, your mother's died, so . . . ? No point spending three centuries getting over it.' In other words, there are some absolutely overwhelming things about death, the void that it represents in his life. He came home, he was married to his writing, but first and foremost to his mother. This is where Proust joins us, as Barthes will have been joined by Proust, for his passion for Proust came late in his life. We need to read or re-read that incredible document by Céleste Albaret, which has just been re-published, called *Monsieur Proust*, where this young peasant girl who had entered Proust's service said to him innocently one day: 'But why did you never get married, Monsieur?' And he replies: 'Well, it's because I'd have needed to find a woman who could understand me, like *maman*. I should have married you.' – 'Oh, Monsieur!' It's touching.

Proust gets home very late, he has to be served – two rings on the little bell, ah! – his breakfast, a coffee, but not just any coffee! The post has to be brought in at six in the evening since Monsieur Proust sometimes gets back at two or three in the morning. She has to listen out for the lift because he doesn't have a key on him. And then there's her husband Odilon, she has a daughter with him; he's the taxi driver who spends his time waiting. Proust either goes to the Ritz for dinner or heads out to check the detail of some dress, to pick up some confidential gossip. Or else it's the male brothel. And here, I think, the story of the mother in the *Mourning Diary* is the most gripping account, apart from Proust's. This was Roland's ghost: my sole support has just died, I'm going to begin – *La Vita nuova*, etc. This, oddly, is where we join Dante and that 'new life', as it were, against a background of sadness. In this respect, indeed, the *Paris Evenings* are enthralling. I'm not sure that *Incidents* should have been published, but anyway, it's the publisher's decision... I saw the same thing in China: you felt that he was really lost... that he needed to find something to cling to. There's nothing more tiresome, in my view, than having to cling to sexuality. It's better to start very young than to fall prey to that rather manic side – that's what it is, after all – which means you go from one disappointment to another. Le Flore, Gide, they're this and they're that, gigolos, and blah blah blah... The Drugstore. You know, it's a pretty glum kind of prostitution, after all... Why not? All the same, it's better to be an expert in prostitution at a very young age – as I was at twenty, since I passed my diploma in the subject in Barcelona, in the calle d'Avinyó, made famous by Picasso.

So Barthes was, until the very end, faced with the fear of total disgust with life, braced for it. And he was wrong, as he didn't realize that what he had done was considerable. He was right not to make much of it, in any case, right to want to start again. But there you are: death was lurking. That's why I find it so heartrending. The fact is, I'm not sure he was convinced he was a very great writer, with a remarkable oeuvre. Because, for one thing, nobody was supposed to talk to him about it – or really read him – any more than they could talk about his sorrow, and so when he talks of the 'writer's solitude', it's very kind because he was talking about me, but *I* wage war, it's completely different. In any case, he accepted this temperament, this tempo. 'Yes, Sollers, he goes too far after all, and Mao and

all the rest of it, phew, what a bore!' We should have quarrelled ten times over! But we didn't, not at all. I think he
liked knowing someone politically very committed, and we
shouldn't forget, either, that Sartre came back at the end of
Barthes's life, with *The Psychology of Imagination*.

It's clear that some things were produced that were not
in the least in tune with modern times, since something
else needed doing: the march towards literature as a way
of thinking, as salvation in the metaphysical sense – the
last text on Stendhal, as you know. And this, too: on 28
August 1978, he quotes Chateaubriand: the 'French are
democratically in love with the level'. Is there still a level,
these days? And he adds this amazing sentence: 'What
seems the most distant from them, the most opposed to my
sorrow: reading the newspaper *Le Monde* with its acerbic,
well-informed manners.' That's writing for you!

There's a uniqueness in his experience, in which he will
increasingly discover (making languages into his subject,
his dream, his horizon) that it may have something to do
with a novel – why not? – a new life, or at least his fantasy.
La Vita nuova: Dante is there, right from the start, in the
text he writes about me, and the myth of Orpheus (with
which he associates my name in a totally amazing way)
remains something supremely desirable for him. Orphism.
People say different things about Orpheus, but he made
the stones roll, he stirred nature into movement, etc. So
there's Dante, there's Orpheus, a whole mythological
basis: Barthes is someone who read a lot. Read everything. *Paris Evenings*, hardly has he had dinner than he
goes home and reads Chateaubriand. His *Michelet* is an
excellent book, people should re-read it. *Racine*, it was
given such a violent reception! Why? 'Why,' he says, 'does

multiple meaning endanger the way we talk about the book? And why, to ask yet again, today?' And our own today in relation to his 'today'? It's still the same, in fact it's worse! Show me people who know how to read nowadays. Everyone's sunk in torpor.

As regards Dante, there's also the contrast between Guelphs and Ghibellines... I'm a White Guelph, one of the few Catholics – it comes easily to me – whom Barthes, a Protestant, could tolerate all his life long. And while we're on this subject, a little detour. We need to bear in mind, in *Camera Lucida*: how the 'punctum' of a photograph is detected. One photo caused a scandal at the time, the one showing John Paul II blessing me, military style, of course, in St Peter's Square, Rome. The 'punctum' of the photo isn't that it was with John Paul II, in 2000, it's quite simply that I'm giving him a book. Barthes would have seen the book; nobody did see it. It was the book I'd just published on Dante's *Divine Comedy*; that's what I was given an apostolic blessing for. You won't find anyone who's more of a White Guelph than me. That was Dante's party. He had to go into exile because of it.

Look at the – very fine – text called 'The Light of the South-West'. It's Bayonne, it's the Adour, and, well, I'm from Bordeaux... Of course, Bordeaux's bigger than Bayonne, but anyway... It's like Rome, which was more interesting at the time than Paris, since Montaigne himself travelled to Rome to find out if the Latin and Greek classics were well preserved there. They were, by Gregory XIII, a sublime pope whose calendar you use, because you're obliged to sign with the date he fixed, so there! A Ghibelline, which meant he wasn't a Catholic, that's all there is to it. Nobody's perfect! As this stretches across

13

the whole history of the West from the various crises in Christianity, and the whole world, we won't dwell on it. Basically, it's a moderate Jacobin theme. Barthes wasn't a fanatic; the proof is that ours was a friendship between a Guelph and a Ghibelline. To tell you the truth, we hardly ever talked about these things.

Barthes's temperament was *tempered*, in the sense of the well-tempered clavier, but be careful, this doesn't mean temperance. There's a real violence in his work, a political violence yet again.

Barthes's violence is expressed on several occasions. First, when he defends Vilar, who put on Molière's *Dom Juan*: there's a eulogy of atheism, which is basically his own case. Ultimately, does the sacred exist? There's a text against Sacha Guitry's *Versailles*, which is absolutely marvellous. A marvellous attack! All the texts on theatre can at times be very aggressive. 'It's no good at all,' etc. So we need to start a review! That's what we told one another. We needed to run risks at the time, in his view. It wasn't at all obvious. It wasn't obvious to Foucault, it wasn't obvious to Lacan, it wasn't obvious to Derrida, it wasn't obvious to anyone!

On Racine first came out in the 'Pierres vives' collection; suddenly the Sorbonne woke up and discovered there were terrorists lurking in the fields, and these terrorists were going to ruin Racine for us. And at that very moment Seuil dropped him. So what did he think after *On Racine* and the fabulous hostility directed against him? That he needed to find a publisher! And this publisher was me. Why? Because I was there and we could talk endlessly, at the Falstaff, in the evening, over dinner, about literature. He sensed all of this, that he needed a reader and thus a publisher. I don't give a damn, personally. I publish myself. I realized long ago that if I didn't publish myself I might never be published at all. It's like the media world in general: you need to seize the strategic moment, or you need to use it, even if it means you get a completely misleading reputation and it stops you being read: but you wouldn't be read in any case, so why deprive yourself of this means? 'Meanwhile,' as they say in silent films, 'our hero had made a quick getaway!' Meanwhile! You can have several identities at once. It's easy for me, I have a temperament that can combine these plural selves, but for Roland, it was difficult. . . The Collège de France, he believed in it while not believing and yet still believing . . . or not. Elected by a majority of just one vote, on his return from China, etc., it's worth noting. But it was a great victory over the social world. France is a country of institutions, we can't forget that.

With *On Racine*, Barthes really got it in the neck; there's no other way of putting it! And he had a skin as thick as a rhinoceros, but he was also very sensitive. Then he decided to reply, with *Criticism and Truth*. There are times when you have to step up to the plate. An example: Lacan in 1969 – he was chucked out of the École normale supérieure; the riot police were there, guns at the ready. He said to me, 'Hi there, Sollers,' I said to him 'Yes, hello there.' He really liked me. There were a few left-wingers; we invaded the office of Flacelière, the director of the École. I've always kept the headed notepaper I nicked that day. I can send you letters with the official heading of the École normale supérieure. There was absolutely no support. I was with Lacan; I was carrying Lacan's bags, as it were. We phoned everywhere to drum up some support. Nothing. Mme Escoffier-Lambiotte from *Le Monde* (there it is again, *Le Monde*): refusal. More phone calls. Nothing. We needed a text, some way round it. We didn't summon the cops – though they'd usually come charging in at the drop of a hat, this was just after '68 – not for this. All at once, Lacan says: 'We'll go and see Françoise Giroud.' I had no idea she'd been on her sofa, at a delicate moment for her. We arrive. A very charming woman, her cleavage showing a bit. She received us in the dining room of *L'Express*, Lacan turns on the charm. The following week, there's an article on Lacan. A declaration of war, eh? I was a hundred thousand leagues away from thinking that we'd get any support from a newspaper that was allergic to all that, and continued to spit on the French intelligentsia, with Rinaldi, etc. This lasted for years: a stubborn, fanatical obscurantism and then, of course, the French Academy.

There was Jean Cayrol, a very sensitive chap, who was part of our common geography, Seuil rather treated him as its own conscience. You have to remember, Jeune France, all that, *Le Monde*, the Vichyist École d'Uriage, all the same. . . It was there, you know. There was *Esprit*, the terrifying Domenach with his beret – no, careful, let's not get mixed up in all of that. With Roland we had a good laugh at it all. That was his kind of thing: he wasn't on the right and not on the left, not a left-wing Catholic, no, far from it! In fact I'm not sure he was as democratic as all that. Nietzsche was on the prowl. And that's why, in my view, it's interesting politically, subversively speaking. He gets asked if he's subversive; he says yes, er, no, but finally yes. It bugged him. An anarchist, deep down.

So, *Criticism and Truth*. It had to be discussed at length. Barthes was fed up with it. You need to re-read the insults;

they should be reprinted. It's worth it, as a little supplement or appendix. Because the tone really was a call to murder: 'Cut off his head!' In fact, the image of the guillotine recurs several times. This bolsters my view that French fascism has never been properly analysed; it's probably much more virulent than we allow ourselves to think, as everything is now demonstrating slowly but surely. Hence my slogan, the kind guerrilla fighters use: 'France is mouldy.' Like a Molotov cocktail, it's being re-tweeted all the time. That's all I've ever written, three pages. It's exactly fifteen years old. On the front page of *Le Monde*. What I had to face the next day!

So the first book that he published in the 'Tel Quel' collection was *Criticism and Truth*. He was looking for a place to wage war. It's fine to wage war alone, but it risks being pretty limited, as has been proven by several great generals who've been obliged to commit suicide before they could make any headway. Or else it can also lead to sombre passions. He was looking for a place where he could be combative. He didn't always agree with us, of course! But anyway, in the collection there are all those titles of his, including *Sade, Fourier, Loyola*, one of the best.

The first time I met Barthes, he'd come to hear a paper by Ponge, who was a great friend of mine. He came, I think, out of interest for what Ponge had to say about language, and probably also because he remembered Sartre's great text in *Situations*, also on Ponge. We hardly got to know one another on that occasion. And then, quite quickly, we met again, we got talking, etc. It all happened quite simply. We just needed to talk for a while. . . He was observant. You can see this from all the notes that he took on the people he saw, the way he perceived their gestures, their half-lies, their errors of taste, their not always apparent vulgarity, etc.

Of course I'd read him before: *Mythologies*, *Writing Degree Zero*, I really liked his work. The portrait of the Abbé Pierre is absolutely mind-blowing. All the mythical little mannerisms of the period are laid bare. It should be re-done every day, but, well, do you realize how much there'd be to cover? How many television, radio channels, etc. There's been such an explosion! You need to look at the period in which it was written: there wasn't very much, there were a few centres of power. There was, for example, the French Communist Party, the way André Stil wrote his novels, there were women's magazines that were starting to break through, because there was advertising, money, etc. There was fashion, and all those areas he laid bare very effectively.

It was his Marxist period. I'll insist on this, as these days it's rather as if Marx had never existed. Barthes wasn't a Marx specialist; he read the texts. . . He had a very impressive feel for class struggle. What else is France but the country of class struggle? Marx's *Class Struggle in France*: people need to read it again, it's of contemporary relevance. Barthes immediately perceives that the class that would later be called the 'middle' class and that he called the petite bourgeoisie was very dangerous. Why? Because, *in the final analysis*, it goes over to fascism. The declaration 'language is fascist' caused a sensation, but we really need to see what he means. What he means is that human beings, insofar as they speak, are potentially fascist. You're not going to get anyone to accept that! And yet it's absolutely palpable. Palpable, provable. He was very afraid of this, hence his quest for the maximum of silence, disengagement: Zen. It's a fantasy, a very linguistic or Zen fantasy, very quick, a flash of lightning. Japan, the Asian lesson. To understand this, you need to be holding a Chinese or Japanese scroll, and reading it, from top to bottom and from right to left. Yes . . . it's a magnificent poem, for example. Except that it's without any corrections, calligraphically speaking. Roland was very interested in this. If you've botched your calligraphy, it's a write-off. You have to chuck it away and start a new one.

A major event in Barthes's life and work came in 1970, *Empire of Signs*, Japan. We almost quarrelled in China because he was in a hurry to get back to Japan, whereas I'm interested in China, but too bad, we weren't going to quarrel over that. *Empire of Signs* – the title suited him perfectly. The empire of the senses is the empire of signs. There's no difference between the way of perceiving, feeling, envisaging, guessing, the way of performing gestures and behaving in a certain way, and deciphering. It may be his best book. The one in which he says the most, on *bunraku*, i.e. the way he manages to transpose his experience thanks to theatre. Never forget that Barthes was someone who loved Brecht. And something essential for him, very early on, was *distancing*: I see something but I see a distancing. This is what he liked in *Drame*. He sees someone who, all of a sudden, makes language into his subject – a really taboo subject – who doesn't pretend to write (because that's cinema – already!) but reflects on the fact that he's writing, saying what he's writing. That's it. And how does that work out as a sensory experience, into what does that transform life? So *bunraku* is extraordinarily important, and the haiku, of course, which opens up to perpetual questioning. In other words, haiku and Zen.

In Chinese, it's *Chan*. Chinese is more ancient. Subversion between the auditorium and the stage. Subversion of the spectacle insofar as it is shown as a spectacle. People want authenticity, you see, in other words everything that always makes Barthes vomit, and quite simply the word he uses over and over: *hysteria*. There's no more vigorous, more constant, more relentless condemnation than what you find in Barthes. Just imagine what he could have written on the centenary of Marguerite Duras! The triumph of hysteria. . . It's very constant, the menacing gesticulations, the social and political threat. I don't need to give you any example from the twentieth century. It's hysteria. It's the 'sticky' stuff, but mainly hysteria, all the time. And here we have the opposite: detachment, not-wishing-to-grasp. 'In *Bunraku*, the sources of theatre are exposed in all their emptiness. What is expelled from the stage is hysteria, i.e. theatre itself.' Haikus too, they speak to him, because – few words, much meaning. Concision. Being able to say a great deal with very little. You know, French is made for that, if you are able to listen to it, speak it, live it, sense it, feel it. It's the essence of concision. These three lines of Basho, quoted in this book:

How admirable he is
who does not think 'Life is ephemeral'
when he sees a flash of lightning!

I don't have a great deal to add. You can imagine it. Emptiness, suddenness, lightning flash, concision, order and meditation. 'When you walk, [. . .] just walk. When you're seated, just stay seated. But, above all, don't fidget!' Barthes always tried to explore this direction. It's what he later called the 'neutral'. But also the 'not-wishing-to-grasp'. Not-wishing-to-grasp is very important; it lies in his experience of unhappiness in love, but at the same time it's experienced voluptuously, experienced with great intensity...

Yes, we should not wish to grasp! To wish to grasp: predation, domination, the fact that the other has to be under my control. He is under my control all the time since I constantly expect him to arrive, not to arrive, etc. How many disappointments that would lead Barthes gradually – I saw it in his final years – to a great disgust with life, even though he was a reader of Nietzsche, as few have been, all his life long! He was afraid of arriving at the stage of great disgust. At great weariness, first of all, then at great disgust. How many times did I hear Roland complaining that he was overwhelmed by requests, babble, chatter, things that needed doing. Always the same old lectures, prefaces, his classes at the Collège de France, etc. What a bore! And then, request upon request upon request... That was the 'great disgust'. What was that period for him? 'The arrogance of drop-outs.'* That's a magnificent phrase. Not only are the drop-outs ignorant, noisy, thinking they know everything, never asking the least question – they know everything, why would they ask a real question? No, never the least question, never the least questioning. A question is interesting; you can reply in a way that's unexpected. The Jesuits say: you always need to answer a question with another question! 'Why do you always reply to me, when I ask you a question, with another question? – And why are you asking me this question?' This is casuistry, of which Baltasar Gracián gives wonderful examples. So at

---

* The French word 'paumé', here translated as 'drop-out', also means 'loser'. Barthes seems to have used it rather idiosyncratically to refer, interalia, to importunate seminar-goers and others who made unwelcome demands on him. (Translator's note.)

that time there was, already, the arrogance of the drop-out. The *arrogances*. The drop-out knows everything, he's up to date with everything, he doesn't need to know. Today, I would formulate it in a different way: the only interesting question about anyone is wondering what he doesn't want to know. So we need to listen. I'm not going to end up like Lacan, throwing out the people who come to see me after thirty seconds of babble, but I do advise them, insidiously, to undergo psychoanalysis.

Lacan also ended up in a sort of turmoil, in a deep state of dissatisfaction and frustration. But what is it that they don't want to know? Where does that come from? Well, it's love. Barthes sought love, in other words something that increasingly seems impossible. Nobody is forced to seek love, or to want it! You need to have experienced it very young, or never. It can't be discovered at one moment or another. It's very early, it's childhood. Barthes lived in paradise, in paradise with his mother. This is the absolutely heartrending side of his mourning, even though he didn't want to call it that: of his *sorrow*.

Barthes greatly admired Maurice Blanchot. You can't say they resembled each other, as Blanchot's preaching – literature is created to move towards its own disappearance – was not turned towards pleasure, to put it mildly. 'Death, and death forever repeated! / O what reward after the end of thought / Is a long gaze on an empty cemetery!'* I'd read this with a great deal of interest, of course, there's more than just *The Book to Come*. There's Mallarmé, there's Sade and Lautréamont. Cardinal Blanchot reigned

---

* Sollers is adapting here lines from Paul Valéry's poem 'Le cimetière marin', and from a song by Georges Brassens. (Translator's note.)

over all these shades! There was an encounter in the café where Barthes had arranged to meet me so we could see Blanchot as war had finally broken out. The balance of power was heavily in Blanchot's favour, that goes without saying, but all the same we had an interesting time fighting in the maquis. And I have to say that I've a very odd memory of this encounter: it was an immediate and definitive dislike, at first sight. He hated me; same here.

At the time, Blanchot was trying to set up *La Revue internationale*, with Mascolo, Vittorini and a few others.

I met Blanchot again at Marguerite Duras's. It was during the Six-Day War – in 1967. In the Rue Saint-Benoît. We were summoned to Duras's. We had to sign a declaration saying that we categorically refused to take part in any of the corrupt activities being undertaken by the Gaullist media. I started to smell a rat: *something is rotten in the state of Denmark*. And this brings us back to politics. War isn't when you lay down your arms and stay at home – not at all! War doesn't mean: we reject combat. Because we have a greater influence over time, etc. Tomorrow the great day will dawn. . . No. So the question was de Gaulle. De Gaulle, 1958. And already, Blanchot was attacking him. Don't forget that I was the first to bring out Jeffrey Mehlman's book discussing Blanchot's extreme right-wing writings from before the war,* like firing a shot from a revolver in a cathedral. I was the man who urgently needed to be shot down. How can you permit yourself, when you're that *nobody* Sollers, to criticize Blanchot in the middle of the cathedral! It had a devastating effect. My charge sheet

---

* Jeffrey Mehlman's *Legacies of Anti-Semitism in France* (Minneapolis: University of Minnesota Press, 1983), translated by the author into French as *Legs de l'antisémitisme en France* (Paris: Denoël, 'L'Infini', 1984). (Translator's note.)

is really long, you know. You have to maintain your bad-boy reputation. I'm keeping an eye on mine. In this case, it was at Marguerite Duras's, and it was a request to make a commitment, which I flatly refused. For all those fine folks, de Gaulle was a fascist. They all followed that line, more or less. Read the letters of Guy Debord; he thinks that de Gaulle is a fascist. Fascism is at the gates. The only person I saw who thought this was absurd was Georges Bataille. He spoke very quietly, Bataille. I'll quote his exact words: 'For a Catholic general, I don't think he's that bad. Look, it's obvious that nobody can be any wiser than Blanchot.' There was a note of irony here.

Of all the writers or thinkers whom I have known, Bataille remains far and away my favourite. When he came into the *Tel Quel* office, sat down, said nothing or very little – 'At school, they called me "the beast"' – it was magical. He was calm, and ablaze with truth.

And then Barthes wrote that little book, *Sollers Writer*, about me. First there was the text on *Drame*, which I consider to be my first really important book. What's very surprising is how necessary this was. The books I wrote at the time triggered such reactions among a certain number of thinkers: there's Derrida's text *Dissemination*, a book that's been translated right across the world and studied in universities, even though the text it's based on isn't. Since it doesn't exist in English, it just doesn't exist! Barthes's text is very important, on points that are I think crucial and that are later found in his own work. It's one of his most metaphysical texts; he read *Drame* very carefully. And he came back to it when his essay was published in book form, with footnotes that are also very insightful.

'So words and things circulate among themselves on an equal footing, like the units of one and the same discourse, the particles of the same matter. It's quite similar to an ancient myth: the world as Book, writing traced on the earth itself.' And: 'Nothing sparks as much resistance as the laying bare of the codes of literature (remember Delécluze's mistrust of Dante's *La Vita nuova*); it's as if these codes must at all costs remain unconscious, exactly like the code of language; no contemporary work of literature is ever language upon language (except in the case of certain classical follow-ups).'

Barthes sees that the scope, the range here is metaphysical, and thus historically very broad, that you're not just born at the time of the Second World War but that you can be born in the fourteenth century with Dante. I was fascinated by Dante at the time. A text I'd just written was about Dante. And don't forget that what can now be considered the standard translation of Dante into French was made by Jacqueline Risset, who was later to be a member of the *Tel Quel* committee. It was a strange avant-garde that took an interest in Dante.

Barthes also wrote about *H*, my book: 'It would not have been possible to write a book so full of presences – in the plural – so open to the world, without generosity, that Nietzschean value.' Nietzsche, very often. Quotations from Nietzsche are always there.

And the title 'Over Your Shoulder'. Criticism, he says, ought to be affectionate. Why not?

One of the things for which I'll never be able to thank Barthes enough was that – again in connection with *H* – he recognized that you need to listen to the book, that I was reinventing eloquence and a sort of oral tradition.

He drew a crucial distinction: there are *writers* and *authors*. There are many authors, but very few writers.

> There is one sure-fire way to distinguish between what a mere author produces, *écrivance*, from writing: *écrivance* can be summarized, writing can't. *H* obviously takes the idea of the summary to the highest level of disgust. It is precisely one of the functions of *H* to undermine the abstract, conservation, classification. *H* at the Bibliothèque nationale ... I'm curious to see how it will be catalogued.

That's how you ensure you'll always have a bad-boy reputation in academia.

Elsewhere, he wrote about me, at a time when I was being heavily attacked: 'Whether we are his friends or his enemies, he keeps us all *alive*.'

And then there was that memorable discussion, at the Collège de France, on 'Oscillation'. This was 1978, and, for Barthes, Oscillation is different from Hesitation. Hesitation was Gide, or rather 'successive sincerities'.

'The intelligentsia is highly resistant to Oscillation, while it very easily accepts Hesitation. Gidean Hesitation, for example, was tolerated without any problem because the image remains stable; Gide produced, as it were, a stable image of the mobile. Sollers, conversely, wants to stop the image from getting stuck.' Have people realized how lucid this diagnosis was, in 1978, when everything was on the point of becoming an image? 'Sollers, conversely, wants to stop the image from getting stuck; in short, it all happens not on the level of contents and opinions, but on the level of images. It's the image that the community always seeks to save (whatever this image may be).' And:

The image is its vital nourishment, increasingly so: modern society is overdeveloped and no longer draws nourishment from beliefs, as it once did, but from images. The Sollers scandal arises from the fact that Sollers attacks the image, and seems to wish, pre-emptively, to prevent the formation and stabilization of any image. He rejects the last possible image: that of the-one-who-tries-out-different-directions-before-finding-his-final-path (the noble myth of the journey, the initiation: 'After many errings and strayings, I can see clearly'): he becomes, as they say, 'indefensible'.

I like this 'indefensible' very much, like Sartre's 'irrecuperable'. So yes, the new battle, one that would be fought more intensely than ever – you can see what things are like – would involve using images against the image, etc. I'm not getting on too badly – as everyone will tell you I've 'sold out to the media', it goes without saying. You have to give your enemies something to do. Make them struggle! And struggle they do – in fact it's rather curious. . . So the diagnosis was, for the time, very accurate.

Everyone has said that I forced *Sollers Writer* out of Barthes by holding a gun to his head. He'd sent me his lecture notes on Oscillation at the Collège de France, saying: 'Let me have them back', in a letter 'Let me have them back, I need to check a few things. . .' I was very touched by that. I told him: 'Listen, you could get a little book out of it.' 'Oh, right, yes, yes. . .' His thoughts were on other things, but anyway, *Sollers Writer*, he was the one who came up with the title.

When the book came out, it met with a very poor reception. It was a challenge to academia, to institutions. And I also sensed a frenzied jealousy around me. It's as if I'd locked Barthes up to get this book out of him. And things got even worse with *Women*, as the book became a best-seller to boot! I immediately sensed that Éditions du Seuil thought that this really wouldn't do. But they'd signed a contract, and some sixty or so pages were read by a local Inquisitor. It really wouldn't do!

So I made my mind up there and then: I went back home – I can still see myself with this, after all, pretty hefty manuscript, next to me in the car – and then I said to myself, I'm going to take my manuscript and leave Seuil. The funniest thing about it is that they didn't believe me. An error of judgement! I have to say too that I have form in this kind of thing. . . Nobody was aware that I'd known Antoine Gallimard since the nights of '68; everyone thought I'd go to Grasset: completely wrong! And then, everyone thought I was coming to Gallimard because of Françoise Verny: a huge mistake. I began a decontamination session at Denoël, as not everyone was convinced that I wasn't contagious, and then here I was at Gallimard, with *Women*!

It's really strange, as everyone immediately focused on identifying the masculine characters in the work: Barthes, Lacan, Althusser – after all, it isn't every day that a philosopher strangles his wife – while there wasn't a single question about the feminine characters. A huge symptom! I was expecting that maybe the women, the female readers, would be furious, but not at all. It was the men who were furious.

A Lover's Discourse, *Women*. . . What would Barthes have thought? He'd have liked it, inevitably. Freedom. . .

The first text in *Sollers Writer* was one of the texts published in *Le Nouvel Observateur* in the late 1970s; it was

an attempt to dive back into the idea of the *Mythologies*. . .
But it didn't work out: at a given moment, Barthes paused
to reflect and realized it was a failure. He stopped. He
sensed he needed to stop. He no longer had the heart to
get involved in social punch-ups. He'd lost interest. The
experiment lasted just six months or so. . . He couldn't get
into it. It wasn't a source of excitement.

At the time, I was quite sceptical about this initiative.
I was of course glad that Barthes was saying nice things
about me, but, on the whole, it wasn't right.

How did we get to be friends, in a very singular friendship,
similar to love? It's unusual. Admiration doesn't come
easily to me, and I admired Barthes. And vice versa. What
happens? You accept and you sense that the other person
is following an extremely determined inner route, you're
going to able to accompany them, sometimes influence
them, barely deflect them, but you know it's someone who
is advancing. It's the pact that's immediately drawn up –
or not! – between one singularity and another singularity.
We could have quarrelled over objective matters. China,
for example, or when I started doing flip-flops. In fact, he
forgave me for everything: that's friendship. Over time,
what strikes me in him is a considerable continuity that
you discover only belatedly. He does this, then this, and
then this . . . but since he has a style, and style, in my view,
is what lasts longest, it all holds up. You can re-read it all
as a continuity. There are more or less important things,
commissions that can be ignored, but, well, not that
many! It all ends up being good. And for this, you need
to have knuckled down to a rigorous discipline: order,
calligraphy, memory – the art of memory. And light. The
Enlightenment, everyone archives it as if it was nothing

special. But the Enlightenment was made by explorers. Voltaire, Diderot, Rousseau, the others: explorers whom nobody was expecting. The 'little flock', as Voltaire keeps saying. Above all, they weren't martyrs!

Once a month, we'd have dinner in Montparnasse. The conversation was very animated, and then he'd take a cigar, and off he went, down the streets, in an increasingly melancholy frame of mind. These dinners, just the two of us, were magical, as Barthes was quite simply very intelligent. And to see someone so intelligent already seemed very unusual!

When Barthes came to *Tel Quel*, the review and then the publishing series at the beginning of the 1960s, he shifted his interests. The period of engagement with the *Nouveau roman* came to an end. *Nouveau roman*, 'New Novel', new this, new that. . . You're joking! The moderns against the classics? No! The classics are modern. . . This is something Roland felt deeply. . . All his determination and his faith were focused on this. And he liked this. Not only did he believe in it, but he wanted to believe in it beyond the 'believable' and to live his life that way. We were interested in knowing how a new *Encyclopédie* could be written; he felt this was something needed at the time. Knowledge disappears: the Encyclopaedia needs to be re-done.

This was when his passion for Proust began, but also for Chateaubriand, Stendhal and Balzac. His preface to the *Life of Rancé* is admirable, and *S/Z* is a major text. I read what he had written, I talked to him about it, I wrote to him and he was, I think, pleased. More precisely, my observations were always positive. This was the time when he started to grasp that the holdings in the library are in great peril, that the dead are in danger. The dead are more living than the living, that's the surprising thing, and the threat would intensify into a raging devastation. We realized this at the same time, hence the path I later followed. Basically, I'm pursuing something that we had decided on: to write an *Encyclopédie*. Given this, it's something completely different, it's the whole orchestra of the library. And here, Chateaubriand, La Bruyère, Sade, Balzac, Bataille, they all go into it. 'Ah yes, of course, we need to re-do the *Encyclopédie*. Nobody knows anything these days! – Nobody reads anything nowadays, you think? They've stopped reading already?'

If we need to redo the *Encyclopédie*, a programme that I've set out in *La Guerre du goût* and in other works, I owe this idea to him. Yes, it's war. His text on the plates in the *Encyclopédie* is amazing. Barthes is the spirit of Enlightenment. He's the most anti-obscurantist of intellectuals and writers I've ever met.

We wrote to each other a great deal. Whenever he had left town, for Urt or elsewhere, he would write to me. In Paris too. To fix up a meeting, or for a phone number... Or for a quotation, from Nietzsche or someone else. It was always very affectionate. They are letters full of friendship. It's like in the haiku, it's *such*: singularity. The quest for singularity. It's *such* a person – it's a good choice of word – and not someone else. In short, it comes down to Montaigne's famous formula about La Boétie: 'Because it was him, because it was me.'

When I received the manuscript of *A Lover's Discourse*, it came as a surprise, since he let various things slip out. If truth be told, I felt that it lacked a certain negativity. I must have written to tell him so, in fact. Hatred is more ancient than love. His book is still romantic. We were two readers of Sade, but in different ways.

31

The *Lover's Discourse* is a novel: it's the novel he always wanted to write. And there it was! There was also the very fine book *Roland Barthes by Roland Barthes*, in the series of so-called 'Writers of all time' ('Écrivains de toujours'). I often re-read the account of what he likes, what he doesn't like, etc. It's the book where there are the most photos, some of them magnificent, for example the one called 'Left-handed' where he's lighting a cigarette with his left hand, or others: '*Maman* is there', 'The beach', 'Youth', etc., etc. It was a lovely, joyful period in his memory. He would return to it in *Camera Lucida*, but in a darker way. But *Roland Barthes* was a book filled with sunlight. And a subversive one, by definition, since the series wasn't there so that a living author could talk about himself as if he were a classic.

On his death, I was so full of sorrow that I wasn't able to say or write anything. I was paralysed with sorrow. On the phone: 'Barthes has died. What do you have to say?' That's where silence imposes itself. I didn't go to his funeral.

2014

The most intense of transgressions, that of language.

What strikes you first of all in R.B.'s work is its strategy. A combat that is unemphatic, regular, cutting, a combat on behalf of an alert rationality, against everything that always seems, over time, to trigger the same nausea in him: the sticky, the greasy, the approximate, the 'neither–nor', the unexcluded middle, the stereotype, the paraphrase, hyperbole, frivolity, critical evasiveness. Dodging the issue is a form of denegation: it is the basis of mechanical judgement, an unthought detour of language that exposes a dependent subject viscerally bound to the reflex that has limited him. R.B. is quite different: he exposes himself – an exact if implicit elegance. He arrives on time, is able to change his impact quite rapidly, soon gets bored, never seems to be enjoying himself too much, remembers. He is the opposite of the noisy academic or writer always ready to talk about the 'business' of the little circle of experts and his own narcissistic performance: promotions, demotions, influences, career. He is not inevitably interested in his contemporaries (and so he does not hate them when ordered to do so). There is nothing of the intellectual travelling salesman about him, a figure well known to us who, having some scholarly 'discovery' or other under his belt, embodies it to the point of anguish, pulls from his briefcase the articles published about him, and spasmodically stage-manages his influence against the perceptible background of a blackmailing of international celebrity. We are used to these rotating and exaggerated forms of scholarly Cosines: dreams of ephemeral tyrannies, the barely concealed desire to take revenge on friends from one's younger days who have 'produced' it. Produced what? Why, 'literature' and 'poetry'. There are three types of ideological exploiters who, automatically, cannot like – have never liked and never will like – R.B. These are: the inspired writer, or 'artist'; the narrow-minded prof; and the scholarly super-ego. In other words, three discourses that lack distance, that lack the restraint that splits you in two. This every-day, oral, intestinal mania is something that Barthes calls: 'wishing-to-grasp'.

His writing is broad and blue, airy. Syntactically musical. Without excess baggage; no useless additions. He is not the kind of man to take a more or less laboriously cobbled-together theory and derive a one-size-fits-all method from it, a Key to All Texts. You know the cunning ploy they use: the basic grid, touched up sporadically and, flooding in from the four corners of a memory that has long ceased needing to justify itself, the 'illustrations' that are supposed to prove their point. Poetic fragments, floating proverbs, sayings, nursery rhymes, reminiscences: the whole panoply of critical cosmopolitanism. Cosmo-*a*politicism. R.B. is not cosmopolitan, but truly and fundamentally *plural*. Are there many subjects as mobile as he? Subjects in whom you find not the *least* trace of: racism, xenophobia, nationalism – in a word, hysteria? The hysteric is the anti-R.B.: the person who ignores his or her other, the person for whom there is no other. R.B. or the anti-neurosis. Let us say that he is inflexibly, naturally, democratic. Everything that, whichever way you look at it, is steeped in fascism, usually unaware of it, unable to become aware of it (in other words projecting it, when needed, onto the other), will inevitably find that he is against it. R.B. versus 'wishing-to-grasp': it could be a comic strip. The French petit bourgeois would simply find himself seen off by a liberty of language: nervous, reactive, bitter, transferential, countless, lonely, he would march along – sketched in profile by Daumier – in front of some vacant area into which he is obliged to exhale all his rancour. His name? Picard, Apel-Muller, Barberis, Mounin – I could go on. Reactionaries, conservatives, idealists, ex-Zhdanovites, revisionists, reformists – it's basically the same gang of raw recruits in a country where academia, which is now the dustbin of Capital, increasingly passes over into its political and economic competitor, also its ally, and increasingly its ideological manager: the future monopolist revisionism of the state.

R.B. as projective test. R.B. as trigger and anti-censor. Reserve, tenacity, inflected backwards, a neutral voice, a white quality. *Aufklärung* white, white-margin-irony, the colour audible within colour. R.B., or self-critical vigilance: what he mirrors back to you is his own self-surveillance, his self-analytical posture ready to detect every knot of excess, every symptom, every blockage. Here we have Protestantism, but tempered, emptied, Japanized. If France had experienced a proletarian revolutionary party open

37

to ideological struggle – and thus advancing Marxism-Leninism, producing its own intellectuals and winning over progressivist intellectuals on a critical basis – there is no doubt that R.B. would have had his place in this party, and would have reinforced his most specific qualities within it. One can hardly imagine him mired in the conformism of French post-Stalinism: on the one side, populist workerism; on the other, 'poetic' hyperbolism, empiricism and rhetoric, sectarian evolutionism and the overblown cult of the pop star. A logical alliance in which it would be naïve to see an antagonism: quite simply an organic complementarity, a system of objective kinship. Dogmatico-revisionism is the natural partner of a manager all the more repressive in that he carefully avoids appearing as such: the liberal mask. Dogmatico-revisionism, and bourgeois liberalism, impose a selective eclecticism: all is permitted, except for the far left; everything is permitted, except for the dialectical exposure of contradictions; everything is permitted, except for China; everything is permitted, except for a theoretical shake-up; everything is permitted, except for the science of sex and its discourse. Dogmatico-revisionism, repressive liberalism, the unity of the *ideological* hegemony (with its reciprocal entryism) realized, after the *grande peur* of May '68, by the monopolist bourgeoisie and the French revisionist party as it now is, and a split paternalist system, psychotically foreclosed, with automatic sublimation, censorship at a glance, scotomization, harping on every weak point in current inventions. In short, the booby trap of the French metropolitan petite bourgeoisie and its hyperfamilial provincialism. France, zero degree: there is nothing more regressive, these days, than this short-term nationalism, closed off from the world, deaf, mythical, droning on, incurious about everything.

We are on the path that leads from *Mythologies* to the *Empire of Signs*: from 'Frenchness' to the haiku. In other words, for R.B., the history of a long impatience, of an angry long march, through the pretentious, top-heavy, decadent plenum of our culture. Through the world of cultural notaries and their obsession with 'heritage'. Through the visceral hatred of the stranger, of the strange, of otherness, of the *unheimlich*. Through a foetal fetishism that R.B. has illuminated and exposed to our gaze more than anyone else, more than any formalist. The petit bourgeois, on whom R.B. has inflicted a severe narcissistic wound, is first and foremost the foetal fetishist, the matriarchated converse of the patriarchy, the bigot, the conformist, the nice pervert, the defender, as Lacan puts it, of the 'law'. The man for whom the Other needs to be *stoppered* and maintained, at all costs, in his fictional existence, as the guarantor of the nothingness of the other. In one sense, the woman in man, the man in woman, the great mystification which means that a basic homosexuality can be concealed under various changing disguises: from 'love' and the 'couple' to 'virile fraternity'; from the sublimated woman to woman as object; from the man in invisible skirts to the phallic mother. What does the hysteric want? (Lacan's question, again): a master over whom she can reign. Here too, the following types are excluded: the woman as man's equal (and not as overvalued or belittled, not the partner of a castrated man, not a fetish there to guarantee relations between men). Man as equal to anybody, the anti-master, the anti-father, the active analyst. Should we call him the player? R.B. writes magnificently, about Sade: 'The couple he forms with his persecutors is aesthetic: it's the malicious spectacle of a vibrant, elegant animal, both obsessed and inventive, mobile and tenacious, forever escaping and forever returning to the same point in his space while big starchy mannequins, fearful, pompous, quite simply try to contain him (not to punish him: this will happen only later).' Sade? Extreme reason. What does Sade say about the obstacle looming up ahead of him? 'A prisoner, to a much greater degree, of reason and Enlightenment philosophy, because he had attempted to translate into common-sense terms what this sense must silence or abolish if it is to remain common, if it is to avoid being abolished itself . . .' (Could you just re-read that sentence?)

R.B. is – was? – interested in linguistics, semiology, etc. Keeping ahead, way ahead, of fashion (whose system, we mustn't forget, he analysed). Understanding before everyone else what the new basis of 'literary' research would be, including for a new sort of chatter. However, the remarkable thing is that instead of trying to impose an academic approach with retroactive illustrations, he thought and still thinks out his practice in virtue of the avant-garde *of his time* (whence: '*Nouveau roman*', etc., the first manifestation of a renewal of avant-garde activity in France, though it was quickly defused, rapidly transformed into an increasingly ancient piece of gadgetry, a commodity for the publishing market in the mid-night of grey eclecticism). Before the Russian formalists can create havoc in the world of received ideas (substitutive haste, such was the void; intensive recycling of overworked profs), R.B. indicates, carves out, and keeps to the correct position. When it comes to literature, he soon notices the technocratic and neo-positivist limits of the movement: he's not one for the little, and now traditional, exercise in phonologico-grammatico-metrics. Not that this is useless – no, no, of course not: but if you're thinking of setting it up as a kind of return to scholasticism, you must be joking. Literature is first and foremost an ideological question, doubtless *the* ideological question: it has its scientific side, that goes without saying, but seeing it as centred on its scientistic formalism is an ideological move whose unsaid presuppositions (anti-philosophical, anti-Freudian, anti-Marxist) are becoming ever more clear. *Yes*, the materiality of language, a certain 'formalism', etc., must be defended against the wishy-washy sanctimonious twaddle of the undiscoverable and the unsayable that are themselves conveyed by vulgar sociologism; *no*, we need to refuse the back-to-school approach that an unjust monopoly of academic discourse would seek to impose, with the repression of the subject, of history, and of what is today's most urgent problem: the language-subject in history. R.B. defends, instinctively, the Lacanian subversion against the old-fashioned neo-Kantianism of grandpa's formalism, frozen in its minimal-language model and unable to enter fully into the analysis of discourse (unless this is in order to reinject a dose of the 'subliminal' in place of the split subject). It is to R.B., too – even though we can't say he has ever been a 'Marxist' – that we owe a critical aggressiveness that is the very spirit (if not the letter that killeth) of Marxism. Finally, and first and foremost, we have literature as practice, process, proper experience, and no longer as the *colony* of a meta-theory. This is the essential thing: with R.B., this new object leaps onto the stage, resists all the attacks of reduction, undermines its metaphysical supervisor, grows, gnaws, digs, deepens. Hence R.B.'s solidarity with the avant-garde need to shake things up. Look at the others: basically, when it comes to literature, there's not much. A few general free-floating ideas about the poetic function and the palpable aspect of signs (but who's doing the palpating? that is the question), but without Freud, of course; a few fumbling thrusts towards the subject of the written word (even Lacan is weak on this point: re-read his text on the Gide of Delay, taking Delay seriously? oh come now. . .; and as for Sade, very good, Lacan, but whatever happened to the mass of Sadean discourse?). So basically, in general, we have neoclassicism or a diagonal glimpse of the avant-garde of forty years ago: these episodes of eclectic blindness might add up, on the ideologico-political stage, to an ideal classico-modernisto-regressive compromise formation, let's say Aragon. R.B. is not historically naïve in this way: for him, literature is a complete field, linked to the other fields of social practice, not the icing on the cake, not the hobbyhorse of the linguist, the mathematician, the psychoanalyst, the sociologist or the philosopher. A material world subject to differential development. A question of more than subordinate importance, a new question, the site of a *mise en abyme* of knowledge itself. What literature has always been without being able to say it? What it finally is, firmly based in its history. 'What is new is a thought . . . which seeks . . . to know how meaning is possible, at what price and by what means.' 'To *change the signs* (and not just what they say) is to *divide nature up in a new way . . .* and to found this division, not on "natural" laws, but instead on the freedom of human beings to make things meaningful' (1963).

We need to re-read Barthes's *Michelet* (1954) to discover within it the disengagement of this historical subject practising language as a subject, as history. 'Michelet's discourse – what is usually called his style – is precisely that concerted navigation which brings together, side by side, like a shark and its prey, History and its narrator.'

Michelet is 'predatory', a musician well versed in narrative verticality, in the 'intermediate states of matter', a transformist, sociable, secretive man. Michelet-organ: 'Michelet's kings and queens thus form a real pharmacy of disgust. They are not condemned, they are loathed.' And: 'The action when "taken by surprise" is indeed a necessary dimension to the representation of the human body in History.' Michelet's books *Woman, The Witch, The Sea, The Insect, The People*... Bataille and R.B. have been practically the only ones to bring out the restrained, indirect force (as far as the signifier goes: as for the signified, Michelet is a thoroughly petit-bourgeois apologist) that is at work here – here, i.e. in the tele-anaesthetized field of today. Michelet the voyeur, sensing the scar weeping behind the historical machinery: 'The sanguinary crisis displays Woman as analogous to the terrible and necessary moult of certain insects; it is an ultra-nudity, and turns Woman into a being without carapace and without secret, as exposed as an ant without chitin, or a chrysalis without cocoon.' We need to re-read, in Michelet, the passage on Robespierre's dislocated jaw. How many people have realized that, far from simply engaging in 'textual analysis', R.B. has, between the lines, made contact with the shadow cast by Michelet, by Balzac, their ultimate fantasmatic resource, the spring that drives them, their 'box of tricks'?

R.B. doesn't have a 'thingly' conception of language. 'Thingly', i.e. with a mentalist or spiritualist underside. There is nothing more metaphysical, as everyone knows, than a certain materialism. The important thing isn't, firstly and exclusively, materialism as such, but how and why it *is* dialectical. Just as there is a politics in Barthes's writing (we have seen of what kind: anti-fascism, strict democracy, as opposed to liberal skulduggery), his practice, likewise, is implicitly dialectical. Theatricalizing. Hence his – constant – attraction towards Brecht. The closeness of their proper names is a clue. But their 'characters' are also akin. Contained passion, feigned coldness, the East, the maxim, the reversals, the transformations, the immanence. As early as 1955: 'For Brecht, the stage tells the story, the auditorium judges, the stage is epic, the auditorium is tragic. Now this is the very definition of a people's theatre.' And: 'It is not some dramatic style or other that is being set in motion, it is the very awareness of the spectator, and thus his power to make history.' And: 'What we now need is an art of explanation and not just an art of expression.' And: 'Theatre must resolutely help history by laying bare the process behind it.' Who can fail to see that these positions are, more than ever, of contemporary significance? Quite simply, we can say that, for the past fifteen years, Brecht's work, through the work of history, class struggle, the world revolution, has emerged *through and from within* the ghetto of theatre, and now occupies a key position in the symbolic field, the internal and external stage of language, which is now neither literature nor philosophy, but is inventing a new relation *between* literature and philosophy, *between* theory and practice: and a new conception of politics too. Even more than in his dramaturgy, it's in Brecht's theoretical texts (especially his various writings on politics and society, which every revolutionary intellectual today should study in depth, without forgetting the decisive fact – decisive in the face of the revisionist censorship that follows, like a mirror image, dogmatic censorship – that Brecht almost immediately recognized the importance of Mao Zedong) that we can again raise the question of an avant-garde literature (the work of language being, if you look at Joyce, systematically repressed by the platitudes of 'surrealism'). R.B., 1956: 'To separate Brechtean theatre from its theoretical foundations would be as erroneous as to try to understand Marx's action without reading *The Communist Manifesto* or Lenin's politics without reading *The State and the Revolution*'. And: 'We must assert the crucial importance of Brecht's systematic writings.' And: 'Basically, Brecht's greatness, and his solitude, is that he keeps inventing Marxism.' We can say that it is against a twofold censorship, both bourgeois and Zhdanovian, that the attempt to make Brecht better known has had to struggle, just as these days it would be against the twofold censorship of the monopolists and revisionists.

So it's always the same, anti-metaphysical struggle against a crushing utilitarian view of language or its ornate separatism: the struggle to link the process of language to the process of real production, to the twofold, dialectical register of history and the subject.

> Revolutionary art needs to accept that there is a degree of arbitrariness in signs; it needs to make room for a certain 'formalism', i.e. it needs to treat form in accordance with its own method, the semiological method. . . . All Brechtian art protests against the Zhdanovite confusion between ideology and semiology, since we know the dead end to which this leads.

We now need to add: the dead end would be the consequence of a confusion between language and ideology as much as of their separation, their split. Language is, and is not, a superstructure. For as long as the language–ideology dialectic is not developed, applied, fostered by a political struggle on which it impacts in turn, the bourgeoisie, the old world, can slumber on undisturbed. An evolutionist, economicist, mechanistic Marxism cannot transform anything, is unable even to glimpse how and why ideology can, in a given set of circumstances, be a determinant factor, a material force unleashing and redoubling the 'final instance'. Hence the fact that, for all the theoretical acrobatics in which one indulges, for all the silences and possible deformations, the Chinese revolution is inescapable.

Brecht already tended to apply the main principle of dialectics – one divides into two – to the space of the production of language, in its volume. His anti-physis attacks the illusion of essentialism, the homogeneity of fideism. R.B.: 'Brecht's formalism is a radical postulation against the suffocating stickiness of a false bourgeois and petit-bourgeois Nature.' And: 'Brecht's invention is a tactical process aimed at reaching the correct revolutionary outlook.' The dialectical practice of language stages the dialectics of social practice, the transformative scope, the operative *depth* of ideology: not as mere propaganda but as a way of making explicit, and deploying, the symbolic *detour*, the rotation-mutation of language, the subject and ideology on the material scene of history, the sciences and philosophical critique. Brecht 'cleans things up', tells us 'what's what', raises questions and leaves them raised (one: the performance is divided into two: epic/tragic, stage/auditorium); in this way, he makes it *possible* for the line of struggle to correspond to its detour, practice to chime with its productive resonances. 'Brecht's ethic consists essentially in a *correct reading of History*: this ethic can be reshaped (we should change the Great Custom whenever necessary) because history itself can be reshaped.' R.B. immediately sees how free Brecht is from the Law, how he incorporates it in a dialectical way so as to disorient both the classical Oedipus complex and the tragic function.

> In the bourgeois order, transmission always goes from the forebear to the offspring: this is the very definition of the *heritage*, a word which has successfully spread far beyond the limits of the Civil Code (we inherit ideas, values, etc.). In the Brechtian order, the only heritage happens the other way round: when the son dies, it's the mother who picks him up and continues him, as if she were the new shoot, the new leaf summoned to unfold. So there is nothing anthropological in this old theme of one person handing on a task to another, a theme that has been exploited in so many heroic-bourgeois plays; it is not an example of some fateful natural law. In Brecht's *The Mother*, freedom circulates at the very heart of the most 'natural' human relation there is: that between a mother and her son.

(We can see R.B.'s irony here in the scare quotes he puts around 'natural'.)

Through his critical operation, R.B. has constantly insisted on the need for a true realism, 'an intermediate state between things and words', which sees literature as the index of a reflective, open ideological process: 'So realism [. . .] cannot be the copy of things, but an awareness of language.' And: 'By *signification* I always mean a process that produces meaning, and not this meaning itself.' He clearly loathes the way subjective and 'imaginary' factors muddy the waters as much as he loathes cheap and facile positivism. What he is obviously most interested in is the empiricist recurrence of poetic 'features', not a phonologism with its bizarre echoes from another era, but the activity of historical discourse, the great investment of constructive energy, multi-storeyed and diverse – in short, the broad and divided unity of the text with its stratified, contradictory subject. The writer is, first and foremost, the one who uses to every*one* the language of *every*one, the excessive particular, written into history, writing himself into it as an anomaly, a knot of incompatibilities, the anti-neurotic, the anti-psychotic, the *impossible* (real) subject that is experienced as such. The text is the vast journey along, and construction of, this impossibility and this disunity. The 'poem' referring to alleged linguistic universals (a typical idealist position) does not convince R.B.: conversely, it does boldly show the way the 'novel' is laying bare the mobile basis of the symbolic function (and here the novel 'incorporates' what used to be understood as 'poetry'): 'There is doubtless some great literary form that covers everything we know about human beings.' In his approach, R.B. resembles the most precise thinker of language known to our age: Benveniste, of course, whose culture is still the most complex and deepest of any theorists of language. By 'culture' we mean here the opposite of what Barthes, as the mythologist of a period of wild modish confusion, accelerated by the decomposition of academia, calls *acculturation*: 'It is *acculturation* that dominates our period, and one can dream of a parallel history of the *Nouveau roman* and romantic fiction.' When literature is really *culture*, and more exactly revolutionary culture, it is literature that bears the responsibility of 'giving a breath of fresh air to the world'. In other words: language is too serious a business to be left in thrall to academia.

R.B. struggling for the recognition of jouissance, a new continent. Lacan: 'The right to jouissance, if it were recognized, would relegate to a now defunct era the domination of the pleasure principle.' Nobody has written in as direct, simple, friendly and *astute* way about Sade as has R.B.: 'Sade's delicacy [. . .] is a potential for analysis and a power of jouissance.' Nobody has seen better than R.B. that 'sadism' was merely 'the vulgar contents of the Sadean text'. Today, more than ever, what threatens us, what hangs over us, is indeed a new conformism, the immemorial dronings of senility – so how can we fail to be *also* in favour of all forms of resistance and subversion? Against all forms of censorship? R.B.: 'Censorship is hateful on two levels: because it is repressive; and because it is stupid. As a result, we always have the contradictory impulse to fight it and to tell it off.' This does not mean that we adopt an abstract position. Rather, we are proving in concrete terms, for each concrete case, that what is generally viewed as 'terrorism' is merely a violence responding to a much more intense and permanent violence, the only *curative* technique to struggle against dogmatism and its flabby double: exclusive eclecticism. This position must itself lead, if it is to be effective, to a revolutionary line. We must surrender nothing to the petit-bourgeois parody. We need to invent everything, sift through everything, critique everything, remake everything. 'To transgress means to *name something outside of the division of the lexicon* (as fundamental to society as class division).' We need to learn everything from a body and subject that are completely new in language, multiple, disarticulated, outside the mirror. No, Sade will not have paid the price of his demands *in vain*. We need to affirm the *hugest* claim, to be able to affirm it, affirm it in and for Knowledge. Have I stated often enough that, in the viscous society of bourgeois Frafrance, R.B. was one of the few great writers of our time? That *Empire of Signs* and *Sade, Fourier, Loyola* were masterpieces? That he had invented the writing-sequence, the flexible montage, the fluid block of prose, musical classification, the vibrant utopia of the detail, a solid basis for what would be a finally tolerable (discreet) transformation of human relations, syntactic *satori*, language breaking into the truth of language? Have I not said this? Will I have to go on repeating myself? Freud: 'Novelty will always be the condition for jouissance.' Everything is combat; let us affirm the beginning.

Philippe Sollers
Tel Quel, no. 47
Autumn 1971

LETTERS FROM ROLAND BARTHES
TO PHILIPPE SOLLERS

Urt
Mardi

Cher ami,

Je pense rentrer à Paris
Vendredi soir. Comme je serai
bien content de vous revoir ra-
pidement et comme nous avons
une certaine habitude du Dimanche soir, si vous êtes libre,
nous pourrions nous voir Dimanche prochain 11 Oct au dîner.
Si vous êtes d'accord, voulez-vous
avoir la gentillesse de me télépho-
ner Samedi ?

A très vite.

Votre ami

RB

Urt
Tuesday*

Dear friend,

I hope to be back in Paris Friday evening. I'll be very glad to see you soon, and we've got into something of a habit of meeting on Sunday evenings, so if you're free, we could get together next Sunday 11 Oct for dinner. If that's all right with you, could you please give me a ring on Saturday?

See you soon
Your friend
RB

---

* Probably 6 October 1964.

Urt
16 Août

Cher ami,

Merci de vouloir bien
garder le contact. Je ne
suis repassé à Paris fin
Juillet que qques heures, au
milieu d'un périple bi-
zarre du genre Maroc-Ita-
lie. Je suis à Urt depuis
une dizaine de jours et j'
y travaille énormément, du
moins quantitativement, surtout à ma Rhétorique de
l'année prochaine; je suis
perdu dans les mots grecs
et latins et ne sais encore
trop comment je vais raccor-
der tout cela à notre littérature, celle que vous faites.

54

Dear friend,

Thanks for staying in touch. I was in Paris at the end of July for just a few hours, in the middle of an odd trek of the Morocco–Italy kind. I've been in Urt for ten days or so, getting a good deal of work done, at least in terms of quantity, especially for next year's Rhetoric; I'm lost among Greek and Latin words and still not entirely sure how I'm going to tie it all in with our literature, the sort you write.

* Probably 1964.

Et tout cela, débordé par le temps car je suis très en retard. Je pense passer 2 ou 3 jours à Paris au début sept, mais il vaut mieux compter que je ne serai vraiment rentré qu'en Octobre, après Venise où je dois aller fin sept. Je vous ferai signe, bien sûr, dès que je serai installé. Ici, c'est d'une telle solitude que je regrette bien de ne pouvoir parler un peu avec vous. Ne venez-vous pas par ici ? Vous y seriez le bienvenu.

Je vous dis ma fidèle amitié

R Barthes

And I'm really struggling to keep to my schedule as I've fallen badly behind. I'm planning to spend 2 or 3 days in Paris at the beginning of Sept but it's best to assume I won't really be back before October, after Venice where I'm supposed to be at the end of Sept. I'll let you know, of course, as soon as I've settled back in. Here, I'm so isolated that I really miss being able to have a chat with you. You're not travelling to this part of the world? You'd be really welcome.

With my faithful friendship

R Barthes

Vrt. 24 Août. Mon cher ami, désespérant de pouvoir vous écrire un peu longuement, comme je le voudrais, je vous écris ces quelques mots pour vous dire que je ne vous oublie pas, que je pense souvent à vous, que j'ai été bien touché par votre lettre, reçue à Florence, bien intéressé aussi par ce que vous me dites de Vico et des différents Nova (admirable exemple de linéarité dans la culture histo- rique, immense archaïque en l'avant (après). Nous en bavarderons à mon retour, ça d probablement vers la fin Septembre. J'ai un été assez dispersé, un peu coupé et pas très tra- vaillant; c'est l'opposant de Prénature, la dans cette histoire où je suis en travaillant bien. J'espère que vous vous Toute mon amitié R. Barthes.

Philipp Hackert (1737–1807)
HERBST. WEINLESE BEI SORRENT
Köln, Wallraf-Richartz-Museum

Emil Fink-Künstlerpostkarte Nr. 371 · Nachdruck verboten · Printed in Germany

Urt. 24 August.* My dear friend, I'm so sorry I can't write at more length as I'd like to, so just a few words to say that I haven't forgotten you, I often think of you, I was very touched to get your letter (in Florence), and very interested to hear what you have to say about Vico and the different *Nova* (an admirable example of binarism in historical culture, an immense archetype of before/after). We'll talk about it when I get back, i.e. probably towards the end of September. I've been a bit distracted, bitty, and not getting much work done; it's the opponent of the Giver of work, in this story where I'm not a very good subject. I hope that work is going well for you, at least. My very best R Barthes.

[Vertically, as a PS:]

I'm going to Poland for 4 days (whence my card) but coming back here afterwards.

---

* Probably 1965.

Tokyo. 24 May*

I'm having such an amazing trip that it's made me quite aphasic; so here I'm having to rediscover the vertigo of literature, as I literally *can't think what to say*; all the same, I'll try to give you some idea. I haven't seen many temples, but a lot of department stores; people have often mentioned you: *you must come.* (There are cheap (relatively cheap) ways of travelling, we can come here together.)

I'll be back – after a stay in Italy – around 9 June and I'll let you know straightaway. I often think about you, here, in this Empire of signs.

Best,
R Barthes

* 1966.

Broadview 833
116 W. University PKwy
Baltimore MD 21210   25 Oct

Cher ami,

Je projetais de vous écrire
longuement, mais je sais pas d'ici
encore par mille tâches, la pares-
se, les ennuis et je viens sans
attendre trop vous faire un signe
d'amitié. Je pense souvent à
vous ; c'est peu dire que vous me
manquez : ce qui manque (à
l'Amérique) c'est vous ! — L'
ensemble est ennuyeux, supportable,
gris, sans jamais un projet de
plaisir et mon hédonisme en est
lui blessé! Je travaille très
médiocrement, sans invention ; rien
de la Schizophrenie féconde que
j'espérais ; plutôt de la dépression!
Heureusement ma famille va venir
un peu en Nov, et je serai libre
tôt, le 15 Déc (les Universités sont
ici un luxe absolument inutile,
pure prothèse de la (bonne) cons-

Broadview 833   25 Oct*
116 W University PKway
Baltimore MD 21210

Dear friend,
    I'd been planning to write you a long letter, but I've
been held up here by endless little jobs, irritations, laziness,
and I don't want to let too much more time go by without
a friendly wave. I often think of you, and I'm missing you:
what's *missing* (in America) is you! – The whole thing is
boring, tolerable, grey, with never any *plans* for pleasure
and this really hurts my hedonism! I'm not getting much
work done at all, the ideas aren't coming; none of the
fertile schizophrenia I'd been hoping for; instead – depres-
sion! Fortunately my family's coming for a while in Nov,
and I'll be free early, 15 Dec (the universities here are an   ·
absolutely useless luxury, a pure prosthesis of the (clear)
cons[cience]

* 1966.

cience). Je n'ose vous demander
de me raconter un peu le
poison parisien, vous devez être
débordé ; mais qqus nouvelles
de vous me seraient une grande
joie.

Je vous dis ma fidèle
et vieille affection

R Barthes

... I daren't ask you to tell me a bit about the poison of Paris, you must be up to your neck in it; but I'd love to have some news from you.

Fondest regards, as ever

R Barthes

19 Nov

Cher ami,

merci — en hâte, mais de
tout cœur — pour vos deux lettres;
la première m'a fait du bien,
la seconde du plaisir, car j'aime
et j'estime Schefer; je n'ai pas
vu là le mass mais j'écris un
mot à Flamand. — Ma mère
et mon frère sont ici et cela
a adouci un séjour austère. Ils
repartent dans 8 jours et moi
je partirai aussi pour visiter un
peu le pays (tout en revenant
à Baltimore). J'en aurai fini
avec les US vers le 15 Déc; je
ne sais pas encore si j'essaierai
d'aller au Japon ou si je

66

Dear friend,

a hasty but very sincere thank you for your two letters; the first did me good, the second came as a real pleasure, as I like and admire Schefer; I haven't seen the manuscript but I'm dropping a line to Flamand. – My mother and brother are visiting and this has brightened my austere life here. They're heading home in a week and I'm also leaving, to see a bit more of the country (but coming back to Baltimore). I'll have done with the US around 15 Dec; I don't yet know whether I'll try to get to Japan or whether I'll

* From Baltimore, 1966.

rentrerai à peu près directement. De toute manière, je suis très impatient de partir ; ce pays a pour moi exactement le visage de la Barbarie — qui n'est pas "hitérique" comme on le croit, mais qui est exactement ce matérialisme sans plaisir, ce monde où l'on s'ennuie, où <u>tout le monde</u> s'ennuie et où pour se "distraire", les gens font de la stéréo et de la cuisine française !

J'ai hâte de vous revoir — ce qui ne tardera plus trop.

à vous

R Barthes

return to France more or less directly. In any case, I'll be glad to leave; for me, this country seems just like a Barbarian Land – which isn't 'Hunnic' as people believe, but precisely this materialism without pleasure, this world where people are bored, where *everyone* is bored and where, for 'enjoyment', people go in for stereos and French cuisine!

I'm looking forward to seeing you – it won't be too long now.

yours ever
R Barthes

Cher ami,

Je vous remercie pour le texte sur Lautréamont ; c'est un texte beau, important, je vous le dis
~~important~~ sincèrement ; outre le fait qu'il change en-
tièrement Lautréamont, et cela au delà de toute nor-
me critique et accomplit de la sorte l'écriture même
de Lautréamont selon la nouvelle définition de l'écriture,
votre texte a — aura — l'efficacité d'un manifeste
qui possède ce que j'appellerai la clarté éclairante (car
il est d'autres clartés), celle qui, à coup d'éclair
change à chaque fois le paysage ; et puis, votre texte
est un texte, un tissu en anamorphose complète avec
le tissu de Lautréamont, qui fait enfin bouger l'é-
criture du commentaire (càd le décrit). J'aimerai
parler à bâtons rompus de tout cela avec vous
comme cela viendra. Nous tâcherons d'avoir une bonne
soirée avant mon départ pour Baltimore qui a bien
lieu le 2 octobre (le cafard va croissant en moi à l'
idée de ce départ). Je rentre dans 2 jours et vous
téléphonerai aussitôt. — J'ai écrit à Seters pour
le Lozola que vous souhaitez ; mais j'ai peur qu'il soit
en vacances, ce qui va encore retarder, et je n'ai plus
le temps de vous faire un nouveau ce mois-ci. Comment
faire ? Nous en parlerons. — Je reviens à votre texte.
Suis-je gavé quelque chose par critique ? "Surveiller" Piel ?
Il n'y aura aucun problème : c'est un texte dont
critique, par bien d'autres textes, est indigne.

Je vous remercie encore pour ce Lautréamont.
J'ai hâte que d'autres le lisent ; et je vous dis maintenant à très bientôt,

votre ami

R Barthes

Dear friend,

thank you for the text on Lautréamont;* I can tell you, quite sincerely, it's a fine and important text; apart from the fact that it completely changes Lautréamont, *above and beyond any critical norm*, and thereby performs the very writing of Lautréamont in accordance with the new definition of writing, your text has – will have – the effective force of a manifesto that possesses what I will call an illuminating clarity (for there are other clarities), the clarity which, in flashes of lightning, changes the landscape each time; and then your text is a *text*, a fabric in complete anastomosis with Lautréamont's fabric, which finally stirs the writing of a commentary (i.e. destroys it). I'd like to have a good old natter about all this with you, and we can – we'll try to have a nice evening together before I leave for Baltimore on 2 October (I feel increasingly depressed at the idea of having to go). I'll be back in a couple of days and I'll give you a ring as soon as I get there. – I've written to Jalard for the Loyola you asked for; but I'm afraid he may be on holiday, which will slow things down even more, and I don't have time to do anything new for you this month. What's the best thing to do? We can talk about it. – Meanwhile, as for your text: should I do anything for *Critique*? 'Keep an eye on' Piel? There won't be any problem: it's a text that *Critique*, with so many other texts, really doesn't deserve.

Thank you again for this Lautréamont. I look forward to other people being able to read it; meanwhile, see you very soon,

your friend
R Barthes

* 'La science de Lautréamont', *Critique*, no. 245, October 1967; English transla-
tion: 'Lautréamont's Science', in Philippe Sollers, *Writing and the Experience of Limits*, edited by David Hayman, translated by Philip Barnard with David Hayman (New York: Columbia University Press, 1983), pp. 135–84.

12 Janv 70

Cher ami,

je reçois votre mot à l'instant. J'allais vous écrire pour vous dire d'un mot combien, hier soir, le lisant dans le Monde, j'ai trouvé comique et pulvérisant votre texte (ou le texte de Tel Quel), avec quelle joie, quelle fraîcheur (sensation renouvelée de nouveauté et de nécessité) je vous ai lu posant d'une façon impeccable la dialectique des trois niveaux : embrasement (et embrasement) qui vous assure une place imprenable et tout simplement la certitude de vivre et de travailler, pulvérisation nécessaire, ou plutôt décapant, car le reste de la page est plein de mélasse ; comment les lecteurs, même du Monde, ne serait-ce qu'en fonction de leurs propres critères (netteté, force, élégance de la pensée), pourraient-ils se tromper ?

Naturellement, la bande proposée par Bardet est fausse, car ce n'est pas Balzac que j'ai lu et d'autre part, en tant que "Barthes" je ne suis l'agent de rien du tout ; le nom seul eût été meilleur car

72

Dear friend,
I have just got your note. I was about to write and
tell you how much, yesterday evening, when I read it in *Le
Monde*, I found your text* (or the *Tel Quel* text) *tonic and
pulverizing*; with how much joy and freshness (a renewed
sensation of newness and necessity) I read you, posing
with impeccable logic the dialectic of the three levels: an
embrace (a blazing, bracing approach) that guarantees
you an *impregnable* place and quite simply the certainty
of *living* and working; a necessary, or rather an *abrasive*
pulverization, as the rest of the page is full of *black treacle*;
how could readers, even of *Le Monde*, if only in virtue of
their own criteria (lucidity, force, elegance of thought) fail
to recognize this?

Of course, the publicity strip for the book as suggested by Bardet is *wrong*, for it isn't Balzac that I've read
and in any case, as 'Barthes', I'm not the *agent* of anything
at all; just the name by itself would have been better, as

* 'L'avant-garde en littérature', *Le Monde*, 10 January 1970.

sans phrase (sans récit d'une action) il eût été la simple étiquette d'un tiroir (le livre); mais j'avoue que je n'ai pas envie de me battre pour une bande et d'y mettre trop de scrupules théoriques, puisque c'est du commerce, qu'ils en soient les juges et les responsables; peut-être, de ce point de vue, cela aura-t-il l'avantage ~~exclusif~~ de l'illusion : me faire prendre une fois de plus pour un "nouveau critique" : la bande sera en retard, mais après tout c'est peut être sa fonction. Bref, je n'objecte pas, faites pour le mieux.

J'envoie aujourd'hui même les épreuves à Melle Faucille, il restait pas mal d'erreurs, et je suis un peu inquiet de l'état général, d'autant que je n'ai pas vu les schémas-clichés, un peu délicats à monter.

Nous avons eu une arrivée pénible : bloqué à Tanger 3 jours par les inondations qui coupaient les routes ; aujourd'hui soleil pour la première fois depuis longtemps.

Votre ami
RB

without any sentence (without the narrative of an action) it would have been the mere label on a drawer (the book); but I have to confess that I don't feel like fighting over a publicity strip or investing too many theoretical scruples in it; as it's about the commercial aspect, let them be the judges and take responsibility; perhaps, from this point of view, this will have the advantage of creating an illusion: making me appear yet again as a 'new critic'; the strip will be behind the times, but after all, perhaps that's its function. In short, I don't have any objections, do what's best.

I'm sending the proofs to Mlle Faucille today; there were still quite a few mistakes, and I'm a bit worried about the final state, especially as I haven't seen the diagram shots, they're a bit tricky to set up.

We had problems getting here: stuck in Tangiers for 3 days owing to the roads being flooded; today it's sunny for the first time in ages.

Your friend
RB

lundi

JEFF — 373, rue Mostafa el Maani - CASABLANCA

Je suis très touché par
votre télégramme (d'
en conclus que le texte
a paru), geste dont l'
effet bienfaisant est
ici inimaginable — Je
passerai 3 ou 4 jours à
Paris à la fin de la
semaine. Pourrions - nous
nous voir Dimanche soir
10 Mai ? En tout cas télé
phonons - nous Samedi.
Amitiés

RB

A. 2014 Souk des chameaux et COMPLIMBIGEAN 15
Armoirie de la Ville
Camel market

Modèle déposé - Reproduction interdite

Philippe Sollers
88 Bd Port Royal
Paris 5e

FRANCE

Monday

I was very touched by your telegram (I gather the text* has come out), a gesture whose beneficial effect is difficult to imagine *here* – I'm spending 3 or 4 days in Paris at the end of the week. Could we meet up *Sunday evening 10 May?* In any case, let's give each other a ring on Saturday.

My very best to you both

RB

---

* Philippe Sollers, '*S/Z*', *La Quinzaine littéraire*, no. 90, March 1970.

Vendredi

95.611.23 - RABAT
Les barcassiers et la pointe des Oudaïas
The Barcassiers
and the Oudaïas promontory
Die Barkassiere
und die Spitze der Oudaïas

AIDEZ VOS FRÈRES
SINISTRÉS
DES INONDATIONS
ADRESSEZ VOS VERSEMENTS
AU COMPTE N°
20-0008-1
DU MAROC

Encore merci pour
l'article de la qua-
zaine, si beau et si
didactique : s'il ne
s'agissait de moi, je
voudrais que tous mes
étudiants le lisent :
tout y est. — Je
rentre à Paris le
19 Mai, ; bientôt
merci   RB

Philippe Sollers
88 Bd Port Royal
Paris 5°
France

0.25
ROYAUME DU MAROC
6-5
1970
RABAT R.P.

Friday

Thanks again for the article in *La Quinzaine*,* such a fine and didactic piece; if it wasn't about me, I'd want all my students to read it: *it's all there.* – I'll be back in Paris on 19 March. See you soon
thank you

RB

Vendredi

Cher ami,

Vous ne savez tout ce que m'a apporté votre texte sur S/Z — d'autant que depuis mon retour ici je n'ai plus aucun écho de ce livre (as letter pour me dire qu'on va le lire, vous connaissez l'entourloupette) ; votre analyse — parfaite du point de vue de la communication — m'a enrichi rétrospectivement et j'y ai appris des choses : vous avez un don extraordinaire d'explicitation et de radicalisation symbolique, une façon de reprendre en allant plus loin qui même dans l'ancien système (genre quinzaine) devrait être la définition rare du critique. Une fois de plus, je veux dire

Dear friend,

You don't know how much your text about *S/Z** means to me – especially as, since I've got back, I've had no feedback about the book (letters saying that people are *going* to read it, you know the tricks they play); your analysis – *perfect* from the point of view of communication – has enriched me retrospectively and I have learned from it: you have an extraordinary gift for symbolic development and radicalization, a way of picking up something and taking it even further that *even in the old system* (like the *Quinzaine*) should be the choice definition of the critic.

Yet again, I want to say

* Ibid.

comme à l'occasion de vos lettres,
je regrette que votre texte ne puisse
plus être inclus dans le livre,
car réellement il en fait partie,
comme geste continué à deux.
Merci d'avoir fait cela si vite
et si bien : je sais déjà que ce
ne sera la seule prolon-
gation adulte du livre et du
mois est elle pour moi un
acte, un bien irréversible.

Ici, atmosphère lourde (car
angoissée et difficile à analyser :
et surtout : tellement peu d'espoir
pour ce pays). J'ai décidé tout
à fait de rentrer à Paris pour
l'année prochaine et j'en suis
soulagé, bien que déjà triste de
quitter certains moments char-
mants, absolument délicieux, ap-
portés par le climat, le pays, les
gens (mais non les "étudiants", race
malheureusement "sacrée" — inutile
de sacrés). A bientôt (à Pâques)
Merci. Votre ami
R

Je viens de recevoir
le langage de Julie.
Remerciez-la.

as on the occasion of your letters, I'm sorry that your text can't be included in the book, as it really does belong there, as a gesture continued by the two of us. Thank you for doing this so quickly and so well: I can already tell that this will be the only adult extension to the book and for me at least it is an act, an irreversible good deed.

Here, the atmosphere is gloomy (anxious and difficult to analyse: so little hope for this country). I've firmly decided to go back to Paris for the next year and I'm relieved, although I'm already sad at leaving behind some delightful, absolutely wonderful times, thanks to the climate, the country, the people (but not the 'students', a race that is unfortunately 'sacred' – imbued with the sacred). See you soon (at Easter)

Thank you. Your friend

R

I've just received Julia's *Language*.* Do thank her.

---

* Julia Kristeva, *Le Langage, cet inconnu: une initiation à la linguistique* (Paris: Éditions du Seuil, 1981); English translation: *Language – the Unknown: An Initiation into Linguistics*, translated by Anne M. Menke (New York: Columbia University Press, 1989). (Translator's note.)

9 Sept 70

Cher Philippe,

Je pensais moi aussi qu'il
y avait bien longtemps que je ne
vous avais écrit, comme si nous ne
nous écrivions qu'en cas de "coup dur";
mais je vois que vous avez eu un
triste été et j'en suis triste pour
vous. J'imagine ce double deuil,
celui de votre père (Wahl venait
de me l'apprendre) et celui d'être
séparé de votre travail — et tout
cela, comme vous dites, sur fond
français. Pour moi, je vais quitter
ce pays dans 3 semaines; ce sera
une expérience que j'aurai du
mal à analyser (à psychanalyser),
à moins de la prendre elle-même
comme une _analyse_ (psych-), ce
qui, je crois, est sa vérité; c'est
dire que si l'on prenait la vie

84

Dear Philippe,

I too was thinking that it was quite a while since I'd written to you, as if we only ever wrote to each other when there was 'bad news'; but I can see you've had a summer of sadness and I'm sad on your behalf: I can imagine this double grief, over your father (Wahl had just informed me) and over being separated from your work – and all of this, as you say, against a *French* background. As for me, I'll be leaving this country in 3 weeks; it will be an experience that I'll find difficult to analyse (to psychoanalyse), unless I take it as being, in itself, an *analysis* (psycho-), which, I think, is its truth; in other words, if we took life,

---

* Letter written from Morocco (Rabat).

, ma vie, comme un destin, qque chose qui se conduit vers ou à travers un sens, elle constituerait une étape somme toute importante. Nous parlerons de cela, vous m'aiderez, comme toujours, à parler et à dispenser ce sens ; mais une chose que je puis dire dès maintenant c'est que je crains d'avoir subi ici une certaine régression théorique, je suis repris par des thèmes réactionnaires (sans doute au contact du "socialisme arabe" (!) et au contact d'une fatalité noire qui frappe tout le monde ici : une certaine absence de noblesse ; celui qui leur manque le plus, du génial trio, ce n'est ni Marx ni Freud, c'est Nietzsche). J'ai voulu plonger dans le signifiant, mais — comme en France — ici le signifiant n'a que quelques centimètres d'eau et vous imaginez ce que cela fait du plongeon ! Mais je commence à bavarder, nous reprendrons tout cela à mon retour définitif, vers le 10 Octobre. J'ai la plus grande

hâte de vous revoir. Votre ami R.B.

peut-être que si vous retardez... je vous attendrai !

86

my life, as a destiny, s.th. which is being led towards or through a meaning, it would basically comprise a stage of some importance. We'll talk about this, you'll help me, as always, to talk through and disperse this meaning; but one thing I can tell you right now is that I'm afraid I might have suffered from a certain theoretical regression; I've become preoccupied again by reactionary themes (probably in contact with 'Arab socialism'(!) and in contact with a dark fate that has befallen everyone here: a certain absence of *nobility*; of the trio of geniuses, the one they lack most is neither Marx nor Freud, but Nietzsche).

I wanted to dive into the signifier, but – as in France – here, the signifier is only a few inches deep and you can imagine how difficult it is to dive into that! But I'm starting to ramble, we'll pick up all of this when I get back for good, around 10 October. I'm really

[vertically:]

looking forward to seeing you. I'm lucky you'll be there for me!

Your friend
RB.

Juan
15 Août

Cher Philippe,

Quelques lignes seulement, car je ne suis pas dans mon assiette ici pour vous répondre. C'est pour vous dire d'une part combien je m'étais senti proche de votre lettre de réponse, vous en remercier, vous dire que si partage, pour sûr. Vos inquiétudes

Juan[-les-pins]
15 August*

Dear Philippe,
    Just a few lines, as I'm not in a good place right here to reply to you. Just to say that I wanted to tell you how much I agreed with your letter of reply, to thank you, and tell you that I definitely do share your anxieties

sur "l'état culturel de la Dé-
rision" (français), ~~ce~~ que j'approuve
fondamentalement votre nouveau
projet _Tel Quel_ et que j'ai
tout à fait envie d'y par-
ticiper de la façon que vous in-
diquez. Nous le ferons donc; je
vous verrai dès mon retour à
ce sujet et d'ici là, je vais
y penser. (Je rentrerai vers le
15 Sept). A bientôt pour tout
cela.   Votre ami fidèle
                         RB

on the 'cultural state of the Disunion' (i.e. French), that I thoroughly approve of your new *Tel Quel* project and that I very much want to take part in it, in the way you suggest; so we'll do it; I'll see you as soon as I get back to talk about it and I'll start thinking about it in the meantime. (I'll be back around 15 Sept). We can discuss it all when I see you soon.

Your faithful friend
RB

Samedi

Je suis contrarié pour
vous, pour nous, par cette
nouvelle imbecillité de
presse ; on n'en sait pas,
ces gens là sont immondes.
Je rentre lundi soir,
j'espère que nous dînerons
bientôt ensemble, ferons
un peu le point sur
tout ça.

Votre ami

RB

Saturday

I'm annoyed for you, for us, by this new bit of press stupidity; there's no escaping it, those people are immortal. I'm coming back on Monday evening, I hope we'll soon be able to have dinner together, and catch up on all of this.

Your friend

RB

5 Sept 72

Mon cher Philippe,

Ceci simplement pour vous
dire que je ne vous oublie pas, malgré
mon silence. Il ne s'est rien passé
dans mon été, sinon ~~vous~~ des phrases,
comme disait Flaubert. J'ai écrit une
plaquette sur le plaisir du texte, mais
au milieu de tant d'affres, de peurs,
que je ne sais même pas si je la
donnerai à publier ; c'est peut-être
un coup pour rien ; je vous la montre-
rai, bien sûr (il y est d'ailleurs un
peu parlé de Lois) et nous discuterons
de la publication éventuelle. Je pense
rentrer vers le 20 Sept (nous sommes

94

My dear Philippe,

This is just to tell you that I haven't forgotten you, in spite of my silence. Nothing's happened during my summer, apart from sentences, as Flaubert used to say. I've written a booklet on the pleasure of the text, but amid so many torments, so many *fears*, that I don't even know if I'll submit it for publication; it might be a pointless gamble; I'll show it to you, of course (actually, it mentions your *Lois*), and we can talk about maybe publishing it.* I can be back round 20 September (it's just

---

* Roland Barthes, *Le Plaisir du texte* (Paris: Éditions du Seuil,1977); English translation: *The Pleasure of the Text*, translated by Richard Miller (Oxford: Blackwell, 1990).

seuls avec ma mère, mon frère étant
en voyage, pour un certain temps encore).

J'espère que Julia et vous
allez très bien, que vous avez beaucoup travaillé : comment, de quoi
pourrai-je écrire si tous les deux
vous n'écrivez pas !

A bientôt,
votre ami

Roland

my mother and myself here, my brother is travelling and won't be home for a while).

I hope you and Julia are keeping very well, and have got a lot done: ah, how could I write about if you both stopped writing!

See you soon,
your friend
Roland

Vendredi 26 Janv

Cher ami,

Je viens de finir l'exploration — une première exploration de votre texte, aux explorations infinies, comme un ciel; j'emploie cette métaphore bien à dessein car vous nous donnez quelque chose comme — enfin — la première cosmogonie d'un monde intégralement révolutionnaire, du langage à ses "références", c'est admirable, captivant (qu'on appelera par une dénotation significative, difficile), sorte de bull-dozer impressionnant de tous les déconditionnements; vous avez réussi — me semble-t-il — à poser une jointure inouïe entre les termes que la société maintenait soigneusement isolés comme des pôles, le corps et la révolution; une mise entre parenthèse nette de tout l'Occident sans jamais rien qui sente le "folklore" ou la "spécialité"; et en même temps vous proposez en écharpe, comme des citations, les anciennes beautés du langage; c'est très impressionnant et il me semble que, quelles que soient les résistances à prévoir, votre texte est un moteur réel tombé du Programme, quelque chose donc qui va faire bouger les questions. Je vous dis cela en vrac avant d'avoir l'occasion de vous voir un soir prochain, je l'espère. Merci et à vous

R Barthes

98

Dear friend,

I've just finished exploring – a first exploration of your text,[†] open to endless explorations like a sky; I use this metaphor very deliberately as you are giving us something like – at last – the first cosmogony of a completely revolutionary world, from language to its 'references'; it's admirable, *captivating* (they will use a significant word of denial to describe it – *difficult*), a sort of intimidating bulldozer to carry out every kind of deconditioning; you have succeeded – it seems to me – in joining together in a completely original way terms that society had carefully kept as separate as the poles, namely body and revolution; a clear bracketing of the whole West without anything that smells of 'folklore' or a 'specialism'; and at the same time you sideswipe the ancient beauties of language, as quotations; it's very impressive and I think that whatever the resistances that may lie ahead, your text is a *real* meteor that has fallen from the Programme, and thus something that is going to stir up questions. I'm saying all this in no particular order before I have a chance to see you one evening soon, I hope.

Thanks, and yours
R Barthes

---

* Probably 1973.
† Sollers, *H* (Paris: Seuil, 1973).

Friday 27 July

[in a note, after the word 'Tribunal', circled in the rubric to the postcard:] sorry!

2 weeks' holiday here, to the great benefit of my body. Before leaving, I managed to get hold of the article on Julia in *Le Monde*, which had been mentioned to me. It's truly shameful, and this manoeuvre caused me suffering, with its characteristic dissociation. I'll try to set things straight in the article on *H*,* which I've almost finished. I hope to see you in August.

Best to both of you

R.

---

* 'Par-dessus l'épaule', *Critique*, no. 318, November 1973; English translation: 'Over Your Shoulder', in *Sollers Writer*, translated by Philip Thody (Minneapolis: University of Minnesota Press, 1987), pp. 75–92.

25 Août

Cher Philippe,

Ceci pour vous dire que j'ai été heureux de votre soirée, comme toujours, qu'elle m'a fait du bien, me renflouant du léger ensablement de mon travail, me rendant plus confiant (et <u>modeste</u>, mot de l'antienne); vous êtes vraiment <u>celui qui aide à travailler</u>; une sorte de grande Drogue <u>facilitante</u>! Pour vous dire aussi que j'ai trouvé une lettre de Piel, ravi du "contact" (comme on dit) qu'il a eu avec vous, bref converti, comme tous ceux qui vous approchent — et m'annonçant que Derrida quitte* Critique, souhaitant "se retirer de la scène parisienne": votre hypothèse d'une nouvelle revue prend

Dear Philippe,

Just to say that I enjoyed our evening together, as always, it did me good, gave me a lift when I was a bit bogged down with my work, making me more confident (and *modest*, as Lautréamont would say); you are really *the one who helps me work*; a sort of great stimulating Drug! I also want to say that I've received a letter from Piel,[†] delighted to make 'contact' (as they say) with you, in short a convert, like all those who get to know you – and telling me that Derrida is leaving *Critique*, as he wishes to 'withdraw from the Paris scene': your hypothesis of a new review is taking

---

* 1973.
† Jean-Baptiste Piel (1902–96) was a French writer who edited the review *Critique* from 1962 until his death. (Translator's note.)

corps ! Mai aussi j'aimerais bien quitter le cher Piel, dont à vrai dire je ne lis guère la revue — mais évidemment je ne puis le faire maintenant. Donc, comme toujours, continuons.

A bientôt, de nouveau.

Toute mon affection à ton dine

Roland

shape! I too would like to leave dear old Piel, as to tell you the truth I hardly ever read his review – but obviously I can't do so now. So, as ever, let's carry on.

See you again soon.

All my affection to you both

Roland

11, RUE SERVANDONI
PARIS. VIe

Dimanche

Mon cher Philippe,

Je regrette bien de ne
pas vous voir Samedi.
J'aurais été bien content
de vous dire la joie et
l'excitation que me donne
ce projet chinois, que je
vous dois, je le sais.
Quel ami vous êtes ! Ce
serait pour moi quelque
chose de vraiment his-
torique : ce pays et vu

My dear Philippe,

I'm really sorry I didn't see you on Saturday. I'd have been so pleased to tell you how very happy and excited I am about this Chinese project, which I owe to you, I know. What a friend you are! It would be something really *historic* for me: that country, and seen

* December 1973.

avec vous deux (sans compter
le grand folklore Lacan pour
nos veillées ultérieures).

On se verra donc à
la rentrée (je reviendrai
d'Urt vers le 2 Janv).
Voulez-vous qu'on essaye de
se garder le Dimanche
6 Janvier ? On se télé-
phonera le Jeudi ou le
Samedi.

Mon affection pour tous
les deux   R B

Encore une fois exaspéré par la
contiguïté dans l'anzy minable
Obs de mon interview et du
babil tout à fait gâteux (répé-
titif) de Cl. Roy. Pardon !

with the two of you (not to mention the grand folklore of Lacan to regale our later evenings).

So we can meet up at the beginning of the year (I'll be back from Urt around 2 Jan). Shall we try to keep Sunday 6 January free? We can ring each other Thursday or Saturday.

My affection to both of you

RB

Yet again exasperated by the contiguity in the pretty awful *Obs* of my interview* and the completely senile (repetitive) babble of Claude Roy. Sorry!

---

* 'Les fantômes de l'Opéra', an interview with Hector Bianciotti, was first published in *Le Nouvel Observateur*, 17 December 1973; English translation: 'The Phantoms of the Opera', in Barthes, *The Grain of the Voice: Interviews 1962–1980*, translated by Linda Coverdale (New York: Hill and Wang, 1985), pp. 183–7.

MINISTÈRE DE L'ÉDUCATION NATIONALE

ÉCOLE PRATIQUE DES HAUTES ÉTUDES
VI° SECTION · SCIENCES ÉCONOMIQUES ET SOCIALES
SORBONNE

54, RUE DE VARENNE, 75007 PARIS
TÉL. : 222.66.20

PARIS, LE 14 Janv 75 19

Cher Philippe,

Je ne cesse de vous admirer — car ce que vous venez d'écrire de l'écrivain est proprement admirable de justesse, de bonheur, de vérité, et je voudrais que tout le monde lisent ce texte et croient à ce qu' il dit. Merci de l'avoir dit de moi : il n'arrive ja- mais, vous le savez, qu'on puisse se reconnaître dans un article qui nous est consacré, et c'est pourtant — hors de tout narcissisme, de toute valeur — le cas avec

14 Jan 75

Dear Philippe,

I can't stop admiring you – for what you have just written* about the writer is really admirable in its aptness, its felicitous expression and its *truth*, and I wish everyone would read this text and *believe* in what it says. Thank you for having said it about me: as you know, we can never recognize ourselves in an article devoted to us, and yet it is – aside from any narcissism, any value – the case with

* 'Pour Barthes', *Le Magazine littéraire*, no. 97, February 1975.

III

vous. Je regrette à l'avance la faible audience du Magazine : cela aurait été si beau et si utile dans la forteresse du Monde, par exemple.

Merci encore.
A bientôt.

Votre ami

RB

you. I am sorry in advance that the audience for the *Magazine* is so small: it would have been so wonderful and useful in the fortress of *Le Monde*, for example.

Thank you again.

See you soon,

Your friend
RB

25 Juil 75

Vous avez bien fait de m'écrire, mon cher Philippe : il ne s'agit dans mon esprit, et je le dis loyalement, que d'un malentendu. Je ne me rappelle pas bien ce que j'ai dit dans cet interview : il m'a été plus ou moins extorqué, dans un café, par un joli garçon (on est vraiment à péril de ça), pour un journal japonais ! Après quoi, j'ai appris que le writing, que je n'avais pas encore vu, avant été linké sur le Figaro : je n'ai pas voulu faire d'histoires, mais n'ai pu lire le writing qu'en toute hâte, cousin du Figaro attendant à la porte ; vous connaissez ces _impuretés_ du métier. Quant au fond (je n'ai pas vu le texte publié), je suppose que j'ai fait allusion à deux carences : l'une, de la lignée de Céline, située uniquement dans le champ tradi-

It was a good thing you wrote to me, my dear Philippe: to my mind, and I say this quite sincerely, it's just a mis-understanding. I don't have a very clear memory of what I said in that interview:* it was more or less dragged out of me, in a café, by a handsome boy (the doom that inevitably awaits us!) for a Japanese newspaper! After that, I learned that the edit, which I still hadn't seen, had drifted off to *Le Figaro*; I didn't want to make a fuss, but I could only have a quick look over the edit, as the courier from *Le Figaro* was waiting at the door; you know the *impurities* of the profession. As for the content (I haven't seen the published text), I suppose I mentioned two deficiencies: one, in the wake of Céline, situated solely in the trad[itional]

* 'Roland Barthes met le langage en question', an interview with Laurent Kissel, in *Le Figaro littéraire*, 5 July 1975.

tionnel du romanesque vraisemblable ;
l'autre, dans le champ linguistique, où
le parlé n'est pas reconnu. Aucune
de ces carences, ce n'était en tout
cas évident, naturel, ne pouvait vous
concerner. Je situe votre travail dans
une autre région du spectre langagier,
et je le dis toujours : dans le sémi-
naire que j'ai fait, au printemps à
Jussieu, les 2 conférences données à
Sciences Po : j'ai parlé assez longuement
de la Phrase et j'ai mis en rapport
explicitement quoi et quoi ? le langage "populaire" (des "jeunes") et votre travail. Je ne cesse de le dire (sinon encore de l'écrire, parce que j'écris peu),
votre travail subvertit violemment la
notion même d'avant-garde, parce qu'
il répond, par dessus la "littérature" à
ce qu'on pourrait appeler le corps histo-
rique (d'aujourd'hui) — et non le corps esthé-
tique. Pardonnez moi de ne pas l'avoir
rappelé ds cet interview : chute qui n'
est même pas censure (il y en a tant
de même !). Ne soyez pas blessé par
cela : je suis profondément à vos côtés,
sans défaillance aux côtés de votre
travail.

Je tâcherai de vous écrire encore,
vous dire où j'en suis (ce n'est pas

très brillant). Je vous passe un mot à Jacar.
Comme l'année dernière, l'autre travail résiliant devant moi.
Très amicalement à elle et chaleureuse affection.
R B.
Je vous

field of the novel of verisimilitude; the other, in the linguistic field, where the spoken word is not recognized. Neither of these two deficiencies, this was obvious and natural to me at least, could concern you. I situate your work in another region of the language spectrum, and I always say as much: in the seminar I gave at Jussieu in the spring, in 2 lectures at Sciences Po, I talked at some length about the Sentence and I explicitly related, well, what to what? Answer: 'popular' language (the language of the 'young') and your work. I'm constantly saying (if not actually writing, as I don't write much), your work violently subverts the very notion of the avant-garde, because it responds, over and above 'literature', to what could be called *the historical body* (of today) – and not the aesthetic body. Forgive me for not mentioning this in the interview: a lapse that isn't even a piece of censorship (such lapses do exist!). Don't be hurt by this: I am profoundly on your side, unfalteringly on the side of your work.

I'll try to write to you again, tell you where I'm at (it's not

[vertically:]

all that brilliant). I'll be spending a month in Juan, like last year; no exciting work ahead of me. There you have it. With my faithful and warm affection

RB

Vrt 13 Sept

Mon cher Philippe, Je m'ennuie un
peu de vous deux, il y a trop longtemps
que je vous ai parlés de vive. J'ai
travaillé tous les jours de 8ʰ à 19ʰ
à mon livre (hélas), plus que discuta-
ble : publiable ?. aucun courrier depuis deux mois : une folie, une schi-
zo — mas plutôt "romantique" ! Je
rentre vers le 25 Sept. Nous dînerons
alors ensemble, n'est-ce pas ? D'
ici là à tous deux ma fidèle
affection
                                            Roland)

Urt 13 Sept*

My dear Philippe, I'm missing you both, it's been too long since I lost track of you. I've been working every day from 8 a.m. to 7 p.m. on my book[†] (alas, it's worse than problematic: even publishable?); no post for two months: a madness, a *schize* – but rather 'romantic'! I'll be back around 25 Sept. We can have dinner together, right? Until then my faithful affection to you both

Roland

* Probably 1976.
† *Fragments d'un discours amoureux* (Paris: Éditions du Seuil, 1977); English translation: *A Lover's Discourse: Fragments*, translated by Richard Howard (London: Vintage, 2002).

Paris, le 10 Avril 77

Cher Philippe,

merci pour votre mot si juste,
sur le livre, et qui, par contraste, rend
la cécité-surdité des autres bien
déprimante. — Vous savez que ma
mère ne va pas bien du tout ; son
cœur est terriblement fatigué, elle
est alitée, très faible. Je ne pense,
je ne m'occupe que d'elle.

Après les vacances, si je puis
m'échapper de la maison une heure,
cela me fera bien plaisir de vous
voir.

Votre ami

Roland

Dear Philippe,

Thank you for your very apt words, on the book;* they make the blindness-deafness of the others all very depressing. – You know that my mother is really not well; her heart is terribly strained, she's in bed, very weak. I am doing nothing but thinking about her and looking after her.

After the holidays, if I can get away from home for an hour, it will be lovely to see you.

Your friend
Roland

* Ibid.

Paris, le *Lundi*

Cher Philippe,

Simplement pour vous remercier de la soirée d'hier et vous dire combien j'ai été ému (oui, c'est le mot) de la lecture que vous avez faite de mon texte, prenant et vous remémorant tout, exactement tout ce qui m'importe, et que vous seul avez vu, dans une complicité absolument miraculeuse *

Merci.
à très vite
votre ami

RB

* en quoi vous êtes le dieu nécessaire du texte !

122

Dear Philippe,

Just to thank you for our evening yesterday and to tell you how moved (yes, that's the word) I was by your reading of my text,* highlighting and remembering everything, absolutely everything that is of importance to me, all that you're the only one to have seen, in an absolutely miraculous complicity.†

Thank you
see you very soon
your friend

RB

† in this you're the necessary god of the text!

* Probably *A Lover's Discourse*.

123

ROLAND BARTHES

~~Professeur au Collège de France~~

Cher Philippe, merci de votre mot.
Je vous comprends, vous regrette
(beaucoup) et vous dis ma joie
d'avoir plus tard votre texte (suis
déjà d'accord sur le / les titres)
~~quand~~ nous reverrons-nous?
Toute mon affection fidèle, Philippe
RB

Dear Philippe, thanks for your message. I know what you mean, I miss you (a lot) and have to tell you how delighted I'll be to get your text (I *already* agree about the title(s)). When can we meet up?

All my faithful affection, Philippe

RB

CENTRE D'ÉTUDES TRANSDISCIPLINAIRES

C E T S A S

6, RUE DE TOURNON, 75006 PARIS

TÉL. \ 325.07.63
    / 325.07.64

lundi

Mon cher Philippe,

Je n'ai pu voir qu'en partie votre émission — et sans couleurs — ce qui rendait silencieux les projections, notamment les Rothco. Mais comme j'ai aimé, comme toujours ce que vous avez dit : sur ce sujet, pétri d'importance, une parole <u>saine</u>, <u>droite</u>... <u>vraie</u> !

Je vous dis mon affection

RB

126

Monday*

My dear Philippe,

I was only able to see part of your programme† – and not in colour – which rendered the projected images silent, especially the Rothkos. But I really liked, as ever, what you said: on this subject, so shaped by impostures, some *sane, sensible. . . true words!*

With all my affection
RB

---

* 1977.
† *Le Musée imaginaire de Philippe Sollers*, produced by Charles Chaboud, 1977.

Vendredi

Merci, Philippe, vous avez
dit ce qu'il fallait. Je ne
puis me décrire.

Elle ne va pas bien,
s'affaiblit, souffre souvent, est
sans doute malheureuse. Les
médecins ne disent rien, sauf
qu'ils ne peuvent autre chose.

Restez là, par là, cher
Philippe, je vous embrasse

Roland

[Written on the verso of a card headed EPHE]*

Friday

Thank you, Philippe, you said just what was needed. I can't describe my state.

She's not well, growing weaker, often in pain, and most likely feeling unhappy. The doctors aren't saying anything, except that they can't do anything else.

Stay there, not far away, dear Philippe. Love from

Roland

---

* École Pratique des Hautes Études. (Translator's note.)

avec toute ma amitié
la plus fidèle

RB

Pardonnez la lourdeur de l'intervention : ce n'est pas de l'"écriture", c'est un Cours...

with all my most faithful friendship*

RB

Forgive the clumsiness of the intervention, it's not 'writing', it's a course. . .

---

* This note, dating from 1976, accompanied the Course that followed.

[. . .] b) This concerned 'Hesitation'. But *Oscillation* should perhaps be seen as different. – Even though I don't really want to discuss this case, because it concerns a close friend, someone whom, personally, I love, esteem and admire – and, what's more, a 'hot topic', an 'Image in action' – I want to indicate that Sollers should perhaps be interpreted, i.e. 'understood', from the view of serious [(]and not just 'incomprehensible', 'disappointing', 'denigrating') thought – of Oscillation → Spectacular palinodes, comings and goings, 'disconcerting' scramblings → remarks: 1) There is an obvious critique of the role of the Intellectual as a Noble, Just Procurator, for a cause: the 'Carnivalesque' can be a dimension in life writing: don't forget that we are *quite precisely* in an active phase of 'healthy' deconstruction of the Intellectual's 'Mission': this deconstruction can take the form of a *withdrawal*, but also a scrambling, a series of decentred affirmations – 2) The *jolt* given to the *Unity* of intellectual discourse (Fidelity) can be understood as a series of 'Happenings', aimed at disrupting the very super-egotistic ethic of the Intellectual as a Figure of the Noble Cause – at the cost, obviously, of an

---

* Lecture given on 6 May 1978 at the Collège de France on the Neutral: *Le Neutre. Cours et séminaires au Collège de France* (Paris: Éditions du Seuil, 1992); English translation: *The Neutral: Lecture Course at the Collège de France, 1977–1978*, translated by Rosalind E. Krauss and Denis Hollier; edited by Thomas Clerc under the direction of Eric Marty (New York and Chichester: Columbia University Press, 2005), p. 132. (But I have translated it afresh here. – Translator.)

extreme solitude (First novel: *A Strange Solitude*).* Note that the Happening is not 'acknowledged' in that intellectual Practice that I would one day like to see described – Ethology of Intellectuals – 3) In fact, through an unbridled Music – without fear – of Oscillation, I am convinced that there is one fixed theme: Writing, devotion to Writing → The New Thing in Sollers is that devotion to Writing (a few pp of *Paradis*) isn't usually seen as the ordinary attitude of *Art for Art*, or of Art + a commitment on the part of the 'citizen'-writer who always votes or signs on the same side – but of a sort of radical panic in the subject, of its *multiplied and incessant compromise*, as if indefatigable: the struggle between the *Inconclusiveness* of the attitudes struck and the tendency of the Image to stabilize, to hold back: for the destiny of the Image is Immortality → cf Annihilation of the Image in the Mystic El Hallaj.

[Inserted in margin:] cf Perhaps Lacan's Incomprehensible, the destroyer of the vulgate.

c) *Resistances*: Very intense resistance – especially on the part of the Intelligentsia – to accepting, to recognizing, variation, Oscillation: clearly illustrated by the contrast Gide/Sollers: Gidean hesitation can be recuperated because the image is stable: Gide produces the stable image of what moves ≠ Sollers stops the Image from sticking. In short, it is all really played out on the level, not of contents, but of Images: it's the Image that the community always wants to save (whatever kind of Image it may be), for it is the Image on which they feed: the 'scandal' of Sollers: he attacks the Image, seems to wish to stop, in advance, the formation, the stabilization, of any Image: even that of the person 'who tries out different directions, explores contradictions, before finding his true path' (the myth of the journey: noble). Even this image seems unlikely, as the scrambling of the different types of behaviour is so painful or, as I have often been told (it's a typically collective malady): '*indefensible*'.

---

* Sollers's first novel: *Une curieuse solitude* (Paris: Éditions du Seuil, 1958); English translation: *A Strange Solitude*, translated by Richard Howard (New York: Grove Press, 1959). (Translator's note.)

Mon cher Philippe,

Comment allez-vous ? Nous nous
sommes peu vus et vous me manquez. Pour moi, je ne sais plus
très bien, depuis la mort de
maman (je relis Proust et
j'y prends le courage de dire
"maman" et non "ma mère"),
où me tenir ; je suis allé
un peu au Maroc mais j'
ai tout de suite envie de
"rentrer" ; où ? hélas, elle
n'est plus là pour que je
sache où rentrer. Mais il
me semble que c'est à

My dear Philippe,

How are you? We haven't seen much of each other and I miss you. As for me, I really don't know, since the death of *maman* (I'm re-reading Proust and drawing from it the courage to say '*maman*' and not 'my mother'); I've been to Morocco for a short stay but I immediately wanted to 'come home'; where to? alas, she's no longer there to give me a place to come back home to. But it seems to me that it's in

Paris que je suis le moins mal; aussi j'irai peu à Urt cet été. Si vous passez ou êtes à Paris, j'y suis — ou y serai — avec quelques trous matinaux, de 3 au 7 et autour du 25 Août. Soyez gentil alors de me faire signe j'ai plein de soirées libres (j'ai changé de téléphone : c'était devenu intenable : c'est maintenant : 325.70.35 : Top, top secret). Dernière chose : le Seuil va publier ma leçon inaugurale ; j'aurais voulu vous en parler, car peut être l'auriez-vous voulue ? J'ai pensé (mais sans aucune certitude) que pour marquer le caractère contingent de cet exercice, il valait mieux la laisser courir hors collection. Mais vous savez que tous mes vrais livres vous

appartiennent. Je vous embrasse bien cher. Votre ami Roland !

Paris that I feel the least bad; so I won't be going to Urt much this summer. If you are passing through or staying in Paris, I'm here – or will be – though with a few gaps, from 3 to 7 and around 25 August. So do please let me know if you're around, I have plenty of free evenings (I've changed my phone number: it had become *unbearable*: it's now 325 70 35: Top, top secret). One last thing: Le Seuil is going to publish my inaugural lecture:* I'd like to have talked to you about it, as you might have wanted it yourself? I thought (but wasn't at all sure) that to mark the contingent character of this exercise, it was better to send it out into the world as a one-off. But you know that all my *true* books

[vertically:]

belong to you. Love to you both.
    With my best

                                          Roland

---

* Barthes, *Leçon: leçon inaugurale de la Chaire de sémiologie littéraire du Collège de France, prononcée le 7 janvier 1977* (Paris: Seuil, 1978); English translation: 'Inaugural Lecture, Collège de France', in *A Roland Barthes Reader*, edited by Susan Sontag, translated by Richard Howard (London: Jonathan Cape, 1982), pp. 457–78.

MINISTÈRE DE L'ÉDUCATION NATIONALE

ÉCOLE PRATIQUE DES HAUTES ÉTUDES
VIᵉ SECTION · SCIENCES ÉCONOMIQUES ET SOCIALES
SORBONNE

54, RUE DE VARENNE, 75007 PARIS
TÉL : 222.68.20

PARIS, LE 27 Nov   19

Mon cher Philippe,

voici ce texte quelque peu démodé. Je
vous prie d'excuser le MMSS, sur épreuves, c'est
plus supportable, mais il faut que je les rende, et
il ne reste que ce double, très "laborieux". — Je pars
3 jours pour la Suisse. On se verra d'une manière ou d'une autre, la semaine prochaine. —
Merci de lire cela.

Toute mon amitié

RB

My dear Philippe,

here's this rather old-fashioned text.* Please excuse the manuscript; in proofs, it's easier to manage, but I have to return them, and all that's left is this very 'laborious' double – I'm leaving for 3 days in Switzerland. We can meet up one way or another next week. – Thanks for reading this.

With all my friendship
RB

---

* Probably the text of the lecture of 6 May 1978, as revised and then republished in *Sollers Writer*.

5 Mars 79

Mon cher Philippe,

La préface aux Graffiti, non
ce n'est pas possible : 1) parce que
je viens d'en faire une à un livre
para-porno de Renaud Camus et que
je ne désire pas devenir le spécialité
de ce genre d'opérations ; 2) parce que
du 15 Mars au 1ᵉʳ Déc, je me
suis mis, vous le savez, en congé d'abs.
de articles, préfaces, colloques, radios
etc : bref en congé d' "Image"
(autant que faire se peut) : je
ne puis sans détresse funèbre envisager
de passer le restant de ma vie à
faire des préfaces ; il m'en arrive
une demande tous les 2 jours.
Voilà. Voulez vous leur expliquer
cela ? En hâte, je vous dis mon
affection, mon désir de dîner
bientôt avec vous, cher Philippe   RB

142

My dear Philippe,

the preface to *Graffiti*,* no, that's not possible: 1) because I've just written one for a quasi-porn book by Renaud Camus and I don't wish to become a specialist in this kind of operation; 2) because from 15 March to 1 Dec, I have, as you know, decided to take a complete break from texts, prefaces, conferences, radio programmes, etc: in short, a break from the 'image' (as much as this can be done): I cannot without a *funereal* distress envisage spending the rest of my life writing prefaces; I get a request to do so once every 2 days. Can you explain this to them? In haste, with my affection, my desire to have dinner with you soon, dear Philippe

RB

---

* Ernest-Ernest, *Sexe & Graffiti* (Paris: A. Moreau, 1979).

Cher Philippe,

J'ai retrouvé ce matin sur ma table "l'objet" et cela m'a fait plaisir : le plaisir d'un livre, d'un texte, d'un "objet" et d'un ami. J'ai hâte d'entendre la cassette. Tout cela, je le sais à l'avance, fait bouger la littérature, sans la perdre. Merci. Je vous embrasse

RB

Monday*

Dear Philippe,

This morning I found the 'object' on my table and it gave me pleasure: the pleasure of a book, a text, an 'object' and a friend. I'm looking forward to hearing the tape.[†] All of this, I know in advance, gives a new momentum to literature without destroying it.

Thank you. Love from

RB

* April 1979.
[†] Sollers, *La Seconde Vie de Shakespeare – Paradis* (Cercles, 'Sontexte', 8 April 1979).

Vendredi

Cher Philippe,

Vos mots sont toujours décisifs pour moi parce qu'ils m'aident à travailler. Ce que vous me dites, d'un signe, du texte que j'appelle "Vaine Soirée" sera peut-être le déclic qui va me faire sortir du marasme de projet où je me trouve depuis 6 semaines. Nous en parlerons puisque nous nous voyons Dimanche (20h au Select). Pourrez-vous penser à me rendre, <u>48 heures</u>, mon texte, je voudrais qques menues modifications.

Merci, Philippe,
votre ami

Roland

Nous travaillons <u>maintenant</u> sans filet. Combien est précieux l'ami qui, du bas nous regarde, nous suit et tient la corde du trapèze.

Friday

Dear Philippe,

Your words are always decisive for me because they help me to work. What you tell me, or signal to me, about the text that I call 'Futile Evening'* will perhaps be the trigger that helps me escape from the doldrums I've been in for the past 6 weeks. We can talk about this as we're meeting up on Sunday (8 p.m. at the Select). Could you please remember, *48 hours*, to give me back my text, I'd like to make a few little changes.

Thank you, Philippe,
With my best
Roland

We *now* work without a safety net. How precious is the friend who gazes up at us from below, following us and holding the trapeze rope.

* 'Vaine soirée', second part of the article 'Déliberation', in Tel Quel, no, 82, winter 79; English translation: 'Futile Evening', in 'Deliberation', *A Barthes Reader*, edited by Susan Sontag, translated by Richard Howard (Berkeley: University of California Press, 1989), pp. 479–95.

147

URT
64240 HASPARREN
—

Lundi 13 Août

Cher Philippe,

Je n'oublie pas le texte pour
Tel Quel. J'y ai pensé souvent,
sans succès. Finalement j'essaye
de faire qque chose sur "Tenir un
journal". Cela va être fini, mais
je ne sais si cela pourra aller.
Si vous rentrez à Paris, comme
moi (j'y repars cette après-midi),
faites-moi signe (325.70.35); de
toutes manières, cela me ferait
un vrai et nécessaire plaisir
de vous voir.

Votre ami

Roland

148

Monday 13 August

Dear Philippe,

I haven't forgotten the text for *Tel Quel*.* I've been thinking about it a lot, without success. Finally, I've tried to do s.th. on 'Keeping a Diary'. It's going to be finished, but I don't know if it'll be all right. If you're going back to Paris, like me (I'm leaving for there this afternoon), let me know (325 70 35); in any case, it would be a real and necessary pleasure for me to see you.

With my best
Roland

* 'Déliberation', ibid.

APPENDICES

Chinese Torture

When our little delegation arrived in Beijing on 11 April 1974, the mass Maoist campaign against Lin Biao and Confucius was at its height – and, as everyone knows, when it comes to propaganda, the Chinese are past masters. Poor Barthes! He was fifty-nine. I rather forced his hand when it came to this trip; he was in a Gidean and epicurean phase, he had loved the freedom he found in Japan, and here he was caught up in the maelstrom, a world away from all nuance. Wily Lacan, annoyed that the Chinese of Paris had called him a 'veteran of *Tel Quel*' (even though 'veteran' was a homage: it meant that Lacan had been on his own Long March, and it was true for Barthes too, constantly criticized in his own country), had cried off at the last minute, with the excuse that his mistress of the moment had failed to obtain a visa. Just imagine: it was a real hassle getting a visa for China. Anyway, I'd finally managed.

The veteran Barthes wasn't best pleased, but as his *Travels in China* shows, he was heroic from start to finish,

immediately bored to death, taking studious and inter-
minable notes on the deadly dull factory visits he had to
endure, stupefied by the 'cementing together' of 'blocks
of stereotypes', what he very aptly called the 'bricks' of
discourse repeated ad nauseam. He had migraines, he
wasn't sleeping well, he was fed up, he was worn out, he
sometimes refused to get out of the coach to see the splen-
did sculptures. Also, he found me increasingly annoying
because there's nothing that I personally enjoyed more
than playing Chinese chess, or playing ping-pong with
school children, haphazardly driving a local tractor, or
having vigorous discussions with recycled professors of
philosophy. I was widely criticized for this trip, and this
was only to be expected. In reality, while doing quite a bit
of bike riding in Beijing, and constantly trying to imagine
what China would be like in forty years' time (i.e. nowadays), I was obsessed by just one thing: supporting the
Chinese, at whatever cost, in their break with the Russians
of the former USSR. Would China remain a Soviet colony?
Of course not. A totalitarian and still Stalinist regime? Of
course, but could this huge country *emerge* from this situation? This was the question; this is still the question. At
that time alliances were being toppled everywhere: Nixon
in Beijing, Lin Biao dying in a plane crash somewhere out
near Mongolia, and always old Mao, bloodstained, floating over the chaos like a leaf, the old Mao of Malraux,
after all, ten years previously. Barthes felt I was overdoing
it, and he wasn't wrong, though he wasn't right either.

What did he read in the train without looking out at
the often admirable landscape? *Bouvard and Pécuchet*.
Personally, I went for the Taoist classics. At no time, apart
from the calligraphies, did he seem worried by a language

and a culture that were thousands of years old and in peril. He was bored rigid by propaganda; he found the Chinese people 'adorable', but the absence of any personal contact completely dismayed him. Contacts? Impossible, when faced with crowds that stare at you as if you are exotic animals, 'big noses' from another planet (at least eight hundred individuals would follow us in the evening, along the docks of Shanghai). Barthes's' *Travels in China* demonstrate this: for him, China was a 'Desert of Flirtation'. And his anguish intensified: 'But wherever do they put their sexuality?' Not the slightest chance of finding a partner: 'Who is the boy next to me? What does he do all day? What does his bedroom look like? What does he think? What's his sex life like? etc. Small collar, white and clean, slender hands, long fingernails.' In front of the magnificent Buddhist caves at Longmen, he was sulky, didn't want to see anything and noted, extravagantly: 'And with all this, I won't have seen the willy of a single Chinese man. And what can you know about a people, if you don't know their sex?' I doubt whether, re-reading his work later on, Barthes would have allowed these words to stand, they are so disconcertingly vulgar. So it was a torture to go for three weeks without seeing a single 'willy' (the word is oddly childish)? And he says it again: 'Sexuality: the mystery remains – and will remain – intact.'

It's true that, at the opera (boring, apart from the women's acrobatics), we might have feared a diplomatic incident, as Barthes was staring so intently at one of the young Chinese men sitting impassively near him. Acting out his fantasy might perhaps have been revolutionary, but not very desirable unless it expressed a confused desire to be escorted rapidly back to the airport. Another gem is this cry of panic: 'There really are too many girls in this country. They're everywhere.' Too many girls, too many children. The Chinese woman, for Barthes, was not on the agenda, and it was precisely this flood of the feminine, 'half of heaven', that was the most impressive event. Was Barthes irritated when he saw Julia Kristeva writing about this question? Her *About Chinese Women* had sparked several polemics on her return, before being published in China not long ago. But all that Barthes saw, in this rise to power, was 'matriarchy', 'infantilization', 'a civilization of infantilized children'. It is easy to understand his sudden relief when we stopped off in Beijing: 'Shopping restores me.'

In fact, the author of *Mythologies*, who had long been considered by academia as a terrorist thinker, was more fragile than anything, as revealed by his moving *Mourning Diary*, devoted to the death of his mother. However, the true Barthes, the great Barthes, is not in these drafts and index cards, but in the marvellous books he composed with care, *Empire of Signs* and *Camera Lucida*. To think he and I didn't quarrel after this unlikely Chinese jaunt! Read *Sollers Writer*.

Le Nouvel Observateur
29 January 2009

Barthes's Anti-Fascism

I will deliver a political eulogy of Roland Barthes. It will be all the more political as we are in the middle of a radical upheaval affecting this country once known as France, a country in an advanced state of putrefaction, where we can see very clearly the outlines of a past that refuses to pass and returns in the form of what we cannot help but call fascism. Barthes is, to my knowledge, the only French writer who, very early on, instinctively – we must emphasize this instinct – understood the phenomenon of French fascism. We cannot hope to understand what happened in different forms of totalitarianism, whether Communist or fascist properly speaking, or in the grey area between the two, unless we turn to Barthes's politics. He became politically aware very young – witness the little group he set up at the Lycée Louis-le-Grand. He was nineteen; this was 1934, the year of the fascist riots. He reacted immediately to these by setting up a little anti-fascist group with a few of his school friends. At nineteen, it's remarkable. But his body had already understood something about the fascist body much earlier, something that deeply repelled him. When I say 'fascist body', you have only to look at what we are forever seeing in the news, the extraordinary vulgarity, the populism that is yet again on the rise, against this background that has never been properly analysed and is always obscured by the things we are told.

The body, too, as Barthes was forced to live from an early age with illness, tuberculosis, and thus to adopt a certain distance. With, furthermore, a passion for literature and for language itself. So, in order to know what we need to understand from Barthes's politics, we need to go beyond mere commemorations, however legitimate they may be. It was Gide, to begin with, and then language. What does this mean? Here we have a very attentive body, one that perceives that society is lying. So we will study systematically and very rationally – Barthes was a Protestant of the Enlightenment – the way the said society represents itself. This produces major works such as *Writing Degree Zero* and *Mythologies*. The portrait of the Abbé Pierre is a masterpiece. *Elle* is described as a magazine that is of great interest because of its symptoms. Barthes goes into great detail; he amasses a huge amount of documentary evidence. It's high-level sociology, utterly different from what we read in today's journalistic fog. It's also a vision of the fashion system. How does society clothe its lies in this outpouring of fashion? It's a very clear forerunner of what will later be called the 'society of the spectacle', even if Debord doesn't mention Barthes, is even a bit mistrustful of him and perhaps never really read him. But Barthes is the first, politically, to envisage society as a spectacle. A permanent spectacle of lies, with money flowing through it, every minute. Never forget that Barthes was, to some degree, Brechtian and Marxist. He and I often talked about Marx – we said that we were the only people in France to do so, with Althusser, who for his part was trying to show that nobody had ever read Marx, least of all the Communists – just as Catholics never read the Bible.

So Barthes was the forerunner of the ruthless analysis of the Spectacle, and this is something amazingly political. I think that, nowadays, he would rewrite *Mythologies*. Portraits, the way politicians present themselves, the way television works, in a continuous loop. The way information is drained away. . . We're in another age. The time in which Barthes wrote was still a heavy-handed time, a time when you could point straight to socialist realism. What is interesting in Barthes's case is that his critique was never ideological, nursed by some hope for the future. That was Sartre's role: you need only read his *Situations*, they've just been re-published. Nothing of the kind in Barthes. That's his great singularity. Everyone was called upon, from his youth onwards, to be on one side or the other, the USSR or fascism. It tore the whole landscape apart. But Barthes was never on the side of one societal assemblage, as they call it nowadays. Increasingly, he was drawn to singularities: he went off to listen to the way people talked, how they reacted, often without thinking, how everyone is steeped in clichés. 'Cliché-ism', that's the enemy. There's been no new political language since then, as we can see nowadays, even though he died back in 1980.

He innovatively used this wonderful word, 'babble', in reference to the Tower of Babel. But the Tower of Babel is a grandiose biblical myth. 'Babble' is something different: Barthes suffered from gossip. He was always a generous listener, he replied to letters, but he couldn't stand 'babble'. I can vouch for the fact that when you met him for dinner, it wasn't to indulge in 'babble'. There are two individuals who have struck me as totally amazing, from my personal acquaintance with them, in that talking with them actually meant something: Barthes and Lacan. Indeed, there would be good reason for producing a political Lacan. All this seems a long time ago. Not at all. There's an increasing gap between them and the intellectuals in the public eye, in fashion, these days, who don't really take an interest in politics. They're interested in political ideologies, which are something completely different. Politics is the concrete art of living, in the present. With the distance you need to take from society, the distancing. This was crucial for the way Barthes looked at everything, and every person. He coined a magnificent formula for today, when we live in a time of violence, ignorance, fanaticism and exponential illiteracy. Barthes would be flabbergasted at the speed with which people manage to do without the whole library, without Latin or Greek or Voltaire, all of which entails a terrible megalomania on the part of ignorant people. This was what he called 'the arrogance of the drop-outs', a great but self-assured poverty. In his day, the arrogance of the drop-outs existed, of course, but it was necessary to fight against very heavy, totalitarian systems. We need to keep the word 'fascist', otherwise it gets a bit confused. There was a fascist fascism, there was a Communist fascism, nowadays some people talk of Islamofascism. I don't know what Barthes would say about this – we mustn't force the dead to speak, even though for me Barthes isn't dead, but very much alive.

Since we're on the subject of fascism, we can't ignore his dictum that gave rise to so many comments: 'Language is fascist.' It's a very surprising declaration and it startled me. To force someone to speak would thus be something that language does itself. And this is very political, too. We have long since entered a society of surveillance, and this gave Barthes a great deal to think about. We are parasitized by being forced to speak. He always places himself before this relationship of force that consists in making you have opinions and be on this side or that. He had a profound love of secrecy, withdrawal. Politically, this brings us to the grip that ideology can have over every formulation. Barthes may have kindly let me get on with it, but he himself was not an explorer of extremes. Kafka put it in a more extreme form than Barthes when he suggested that the truth could destroy nothing except what had been destroyed. Barthes felt this very intensely, being very sensitive as he was to the question of death. His mother's death was a cataclysm; the *Mourning Diary* is very moving. All this intensified by the drama that would have occurred if his mother had learned about his homosexuality. This is what we might call a certain political limit in Barthes. This doesn't mean – quite the contrary – that he should have been an activist, a failure of which gay activists often accuse him. This isn't the way Barthes viewed his own homosexuality, which was always tinged with a desire that as often as not was left unsatisfied. But it's a political question and we're in the thick of it now, with marriage for all, assisted reproductive technology, etc. What would he have had to say about this? I don't know, but I do know that he would definitely have taken a great interest in the way contemporary society lies to itself through the ways it spreads information and rapidly evaporating news.

In conversation with
Josyane Savigneau,
Le Monde,
'Roland Barthes, l'Inattendu', special issue, 2015